MARMOL RADZINER + ASSOCIATES

MARMOL RADZINER + ASSOCIATES
BETWEEN ARCHITECTURE AND CONSTRUCTION

Leo Marmol FAIA and Ron Radziner FAIA
Foreword by Paul Goldberger
Edited by Karen Weise

Princeton Architectural Press, New York

Published by
Princeton Architectural Press
37 East Seventh Street
New York, New York 10003

For a free catalog of books, call 1.800.722.6657.
Visit our web site at www.papress.com.

Art direction: Lorraine Wild and Robin Cottle
Design: Annessa Braymer and Victor Hu, Green Dragon Office, Los Angeles
Editor: Lauren Nelson Packard

Special thanks to:
Karen Weise, Robin Cottle, Alicia Daugherty, Paul Goldberger, Lorraine Wild,
Annessa Braymer, Victor Hu, Anna Hill, Coralie Langston-Jones and Lauren Nelson
Packard for their thoughtful design and editorial contribution to this book
— Marmol Radziner and Associates

Nettie Aljian, Sara Bader, Dorothy Ball, Nicola Bednarek, Janet Behning,
Becca Casbon, Penny (Yuen Pik) Chu, Russell Fernandez, Pete Fitzpatrick,
Wendy Fuller, Jan Haux, Clare Jacobson, Aileen Kwun, Nancy Eklund Later, Linda Lee,
Laurie Manfra, Katharine Myers, Jennifer Thompson, Arnoud Verhage, Paul Wagner,
Joseph Weston, and Deb Wood of Princeton Architectural Press
—Kevin C. Lippert, publisher

Library of Congress Cataloging-in-Publication Data
Marmol, Leo.
   Marmol Radziner + Associates : between architecture and
construction / Leo Marmol, Ron Radziner.
      p. cm.
   ISBN 978-1-56898-744-6 (alk. paper)
   1. Marmol Radziner + Associates. 2. Architecture—
California—20th century. 3. Architecture—California—21st
century. I. Radziner, Ron. II. Title.
   NA737.M2168A4 2008
   720.92'2--dc22
                        2008002877

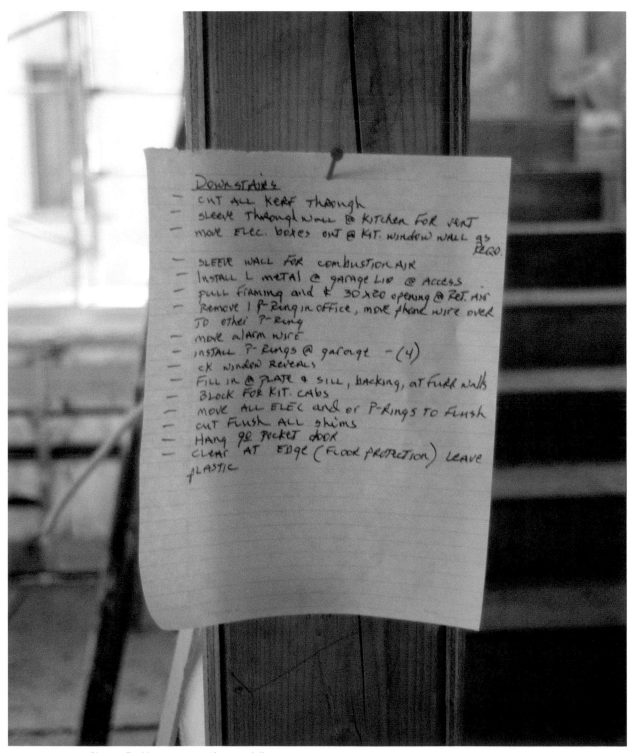

Glencoe Residence construction punch list

FOREWORD   I first encountered Leo Marmol and Ron Radziner the same way a lot of people did, through their remarkable restoration of Richard Neutra's great Edgar Kaufmann House in Palm Springs. When I heard about the project I had no idea how a relatively young pair of architects from Santa Monica had ended up with the job of bringing back one of the great modernist houses of the twentieth century from decades of architectural abuse. All I knew was that they had figured out how to return it to something approximating its appearance in 1947, when Julius Shulman took his celebrated photograph of the house at dusk, with the reclining figure of Lillian Kaufmann, the curves of the chaise lounges, and the profile of the mountains all in precise counterpoint to the pristine lines of Neutra's architecture. Shulman's exquisitely composed image defined the Kaufmann House for me as it did for most people who knew this house only through photographs. I had no idea how much the real Kaufmann House had been altered by unsympathetic later owners, and how by the early 1990s, it bore only moderate resemblance to the iconic house that, thanks to Shulman, all of us had in our heads. Then the house's luck changed. First, in 1992 it was purchased by Beth and Brent Harris, a couple who bought the house not for where it was but for what it was, and set out to restore it. And then Beth Harris, an architectural historian, decided that Marmol and Radziner were the people to take charge of the job.

She was taking a leap of faith, since Marmol Radziner + Associates hadn't done a restoration project like this. But then again, no one else had either. In 1992, modernist preservation was not yet a hot topic, and almost no one could claim any significant experience in restoring modern buildings at all, let alone in rehabilitating a house that was a modernist masterpiece. Several architectural firms that specialized in historic preservation had turned the job down when Harris, who was increasingly frustrated at the difficulty of finding an architect who shared her belief that the house could be brought back to its original appearance, was given Marmol Radziner + Associates' name by a colleague. She hadn't heard of them either. But it did not take her long to figure out that they were talented architects who possessed two things Harris knew were essential: a strong predisposition, not to say a passion, for twentieth-century modernism, and a lot of experience in construction. Marmol and Radziner's small firm had begun to establish itself as a "design-build" contracting team, and they had been building their reputation as architects who cared not only about how things looked but about how they were put together. Harris hired them; it took five years; the absence of full documentation meant that Julius Shulman's photographs and interviews with people who had worked on the original house turned out to be critical. That story has been well told by now. The key thing is the willingness, even the excitement, that Marmol and Radziner felt at combining historical research with technical judgments. What would Richard Neutra have done? How to embrace new technologies and new materials while being true to the look of the house? They seem to have reveled in the challenge of it all.

Marmol Radziner + Associates was rewarded with the commission to design a new pool house for the Harrises, to sit at the far end of the property from the original house. This posed a design dilemma of a different sort. It could not be the same as the Kaufmann House, since to openly mimic the work of the master that you have been trying to save would be trite, and Marmol and Radziner knew it. Yet the pool house could not be so different that it would appear out of place, and Marmol and Radziner knew this, too. Either way, they risked undercutting the restoration and appearing to violate the spirit of the house.

The success with which they solved this problem stands as a reminder that they are good at much more than paying homage to modernist masters. The pool house is Neutra-esque without being Neutra-like. It subtly echoes themes of the main house but with different proportions, a slightly different palette of materials, and a sense, overall, of being at once heavier than the original house and newer. The pool house is responsive to the Neutra house without being competitive with it, and it is graceful on its own terms.

Change "Neutra house" to "the modernist tradition," and you could say the same thing about all of Marmol Radziner + Associates' architecture. It is sympathetic to the International Style without being slavishly imitative. Their buildings—and I think particularly of Ron Radziner's two houses for his family (Glencoe and Vienna Way Residences), as well as the Ward Luu House in Rustic Canyon and the Hilltop Studio in Pasadena—are elegant, but they are more than that. They sit on the land with an ease that makes you think that they have a bit of Frank Lloyd Wright in their genetic makeup along with the International Style. And those Marmol Radziner + Associates buildings that address the street suggest that these architects possess a comfort with urbanism that goes well beyond anything their modernist forebears had and a desire to reconcile modernism's historic indifference to the street and, indeed, to the whole fabric of the existing city.

Marmol and Radziner also far exceed the early modernists in their commitment to social responsibility and technology, both areas in which the early modern architects talked a good game but accomplished far less. Their Accelerated School of South Los Angeles and Flight Child Developmental Center at Los Angeles International Airport, among other projects, make it clear that they do not want only to design houses for the rich, and how determined they are to prove that serious modern architecture can work in a social context. But when all is said and done, Marmol Radziner + Associates may make their broadest impact through their remarkable series of prefabricated modernist houses, which emerges not only out of the aesthetic of their other work, but also from their deep understanding of building technology and construction methods. Here, too, there is social responsibility—this is a system devised to bring the high modernist aesthetic to people who could never afford to commission a custom house—but there is also an eagerness to show how flexible, and also how beautiful, such architecture can be when factory-made. Leo Marmol's own Desert House served as a prototype, and it is hard to imagine a prefab house being more alluring. It possesses all of the elegance and all of the strength of the aesthetic that Marmol and Radziner pursue in their other projects, an aesthetic that is deeply connected to classic International Style modernism without being constrained by it. The debt they owe to the Barcelona Pavilion is incalculable, surely. But they repay it, building by building, by being consistently inventive, as if they were intent on proving that their models are forever vital, sources of fresh ideas still.

—Paul Goldberger

Introduction

We are architects first and foremost. Seeing construction as the work that supports our architecture, we approach projects from an integrative perspective that accepts the responsibilities and challenges of constructing the ideas that we design. Our design-build practice creates a dedicated, rigorous, and often messy process. With this book, we hope to provide a window into how we try to make design-build work.

Since we started our practice in 1989, we have found ourselves bringing larger and larger projects in-house, starting with the early development of our construction staff through the recent opening of our own prefab factory. Trying to reclaim control of the craft and implementation of our designs, we confront problems normally not considered in a traditional architectural practice—issues of material availability, ease of execution, the labor environment, and weather fluctuation. In reality it has come down to dealing with torrential rain, chronically tardy subcontractors, fist-fights between construction staff, and material delays due to hurricanes.

For decades, a design-build approach such as ours was considered unethical. From its founding in 1857 until 1979, the American Institute of Architects (AIA) banned design-build practices due to a potential conflict of interest. The AIA defined architecture as something separate from building and developed standardized contracts that put architects in charge of the overall process. Many in our profession have lost respect for making objects, which we find counterintuitive, because architecture is about the object. While a standard concern of design-build is that architects hold back on designs when they know they are responsible for building, we find the opposite to be the case. We challenge ourselves as crafts-people and builders to take the rigor of desiging a project and extend it into the execution of complex conditions.

Our design-build approach is inspired by historic models of the "master builder" and, like the Bauhaus, is oriented both toward a modern and a craft tradition. We strive to link creative design fields in an experimental process of making physical spaces that embrace nature, respond to the surround-ing context, and extend the design process into the craft of production. Whenever possible, we integrate architecture, custom furniture, interior design, landscape design, and fabrication to create cohesive design solutions. With our contemporary culture of visual chaos and complexity, we recognize the ideals of modernism—of simplification, respect for materials, and integration with nature—as a way of providing calm and inspiration. All of our projects, from small, intimately scaled residences to large urban campuses, merge indoor and outdoor spaces to create environments where families flourish, ideas prosper, and communities gather.

With nearly fifty architectural, forty construction, and eighty prefab staff members, our firm is full of craftspeople. We employ welders who trained as architects, architects who worked on construction sites, and everything in between. We appreciate the wide range of people responsible for making a project possible. From the supportive client to the master mason, we know the power of collaboration. For this book, we've asked over forty people, including clients, architects, construction staff, subcontractors, and colleagues, to reflect on current and past projects in hopes of revealing the give and take between the ideals of design and the reality of building.

Woodley Residence construction

EARLY CLIENT RELATIONSHIPS

"At the time, it was so unique to people that we were architects who were also contractors. Here were two trained architects who could sit down and talk about the construction of a building, issues of detailing, and how to fix something. People really felt blessed that they could have a conversation about all aspects of a home from design through construction. We were working with smaller budgets, and the projects were really big investments for these families. They wanted to make sure that it was going to be done right and that they were working with people they could trust. When we were struggling for work, it was very reassuring to know that we had clients who supported what the firm did and what we represented. They were willing to take a chance on us. I think many of our early clients are proud that they were pioneers who took the first plunge into hiring us to be the contractor. Our clients now don't think twice about the fact that we are architects and contractors."
—*Chris Shanley, Senior Associate*

Our practice started out, very unglamorously, with garage additions, bathroom renovations and alterations to industrial buildings. Through all of the early projects, our biggest challenge was having our designs built properly. When working with tight budgets, we grappled with how to make something architecturally strong while also ensuring that the project would come to fruition. We became very interested in the potential of integrating the design and construction aspects of creating a space. We wanted to establish that doing construction and architecture together was a legitimate, and perhaps better, way for us to work.

Early on, we worked on projects with varying degrees of on-site involvement. On the residential side, we had projects like the McCullough Residence addition, where we worked closely with the owner-builder in coordinating construction. We also worked on the Rosenfeld Residence, an addition designed as a series of boxes and bridges on top of an old Venice bungalow. On the institutional side, we collaborated with Michael Maltzan on the nonprofit arts school, Mark Taper Center/Inner City Arts, located in downtown Los Angeles. This project taught us the technicalities of retrofitting an old, industrial building for a completely new use.

Our early projects were all small in scale, so the general contractors often available to us were not as sophisticated as we had hoped. Over and over again, we were disappointed. We produced detailed architectural drawings that the contractors ignored. In order to get projects built correctly, we guided the contractors on a daily basis. Our continued frustration by this lack of control was the inspiration for us to become the general contractors ourselves.

Rosenfeld Residence

Rosenfeld Residence

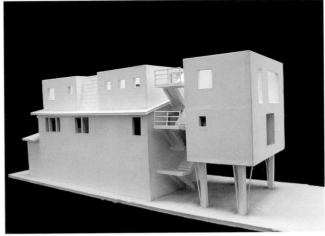

Mark Taper Center/Inner City Arts

Rustic Canyon Residence

Rustic Canyon Residence

EARLY CONSTRUCTION

"One of the early building projects was a deck for a family in Santa Monica Canyon. That was only a three or four week job, and it happened in the middle of winter. We spent as much time covering and uncovering the roof in plastic as anything else. One of the roofers fell through the roof and landed in the living room, while the client was sitting right there."
—*Scott Enge, Site Supervisor*

"I started in 1997 working on the Rustic Canyon Residence. I came in as a handyman for the site super. I was shocked because this was my first encounter with these high-end homes. It was pretty intense because it was subterranean, and we were in ditches all the time. It was months of hell. There were a lot of rainy days back in the fall of '97. There was water everywhere. Just try waterproofing and backfilling in a rainy season."
—*Hubert Plunkett, Construction Labor Staff*

Our first project in which we acted both as the architect and contractor, the Woodley Residence, was an important turning point for our small practice. The thought of building an entire house was both daunting and exciting. At that time, in the early 1990s, Southern California was in the midst of a housing slump, so we were just happy to have work. The construction process was very homegrown. We hauled the construction waste to the dump ourselves every weekend, and we employed various unemployed architect friends as laborers. Leo was on site each day as the superintendent, and Chris Shanley, now our Senior Associate, spent his first several weeks at the firm painting the home. We endured erratic subcontractors, including a cursing framer who hurled lumber and obscenities all over the site, and disappearing electricians, who abruptly left for Florida to take advantage of the lucrative work left in Hurricane Andrew's wake. As we saw it, everything that we could do ourselves was money we didn't have to pay someone else and was one fewer subcontractor to wrangle. We also welcomed the opportunity to dive into the nuts and bolts of building a difficult home on a restrictive site. Today, it is difficult for our staff and clients to imagine the two of us wearing tool belts and digging ditches, but that is indeed how we started.

Despite the chaos of Woodley, we kept pursuing design-build opportunities wherever possible to learn more about architecture and construction. By the time we started the Rustic Canyon Residence in 1996, we were able to staff the construction site with much of our own full-time labor. The home was a complex challenge both to design and build, for it quadrupled the size of a small clapboard cottage set in an Oak grove on a steep hillside. We integrated the traditional style of the original cottage with modern materials, such as board-formed concrete and Cor-Ten steel. A deep excavation and significant subterranean construction

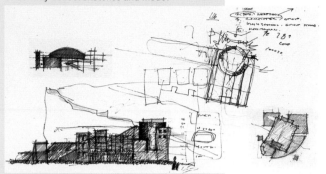

Sheenway School sketches and model

SHEENWAY SCHOOL

Following the Los Angeles riots, we became involved in designing a new private school in South Central Los Angeles. We supported the way the founder of the Sheenway School, Dolores Sheen, envisioned solving inner-city issues. The school had an integrated program, combining a school for kindergarten through twelfth grade on the same site with housing for the elderly, community gardens, and retail spaces like a food cooperative. Beyond spending months developing the design, we engaged with the school, teaching classes, painting their existing buildings and making pancakes. This ambitious program was too progressive for its time and never raised the funds necessary to proceed. Years later we put these ideas of a programmatically integrated urban school to the test in our design of The Accelerated School of South Los Angeles.

was necessary for the addition to climb and wrap around the existing oaks. Since the site was so steep, our construction staff walked around the excavation sites with ropes tied around their waists, as if rappelling down a cliff. While much of the work was done by our own construction staff, somehow we managed to end up with that same swearing framer. On this project, we learned first-hand about a wide swath of trades, from subsurface waterproofing to building forms for concrete.

These new skills became essential in our first forays into restoring iconic modern homes. A friend of ours worked for Frank Gehry's office and knew we were interested in combining design and construction. Since we were looking to bring in new work, he referred us to some of his office's former clients with houses that were leaking. With these innovative and influential homes, we dove into the technicalities of waterproofing peculiar conditions. We spent several weeks testing to determine the exact location of the technical failures and then designed and built solutions that repaired the home without changing the aesthetics of the sculptural architectural forms. Looking at the leaky home, we could not help but perceive that the shortcomings of a traditional architect-contractor relationship let down the wonderful, daring architectural concepts. On these homes, we were able both to design and then build the careful details necessary to protect the original design from the destructive intrusion of water. We completed the projects with improved technical skills and a reinforced belief in the benefits of integrating design and construction.

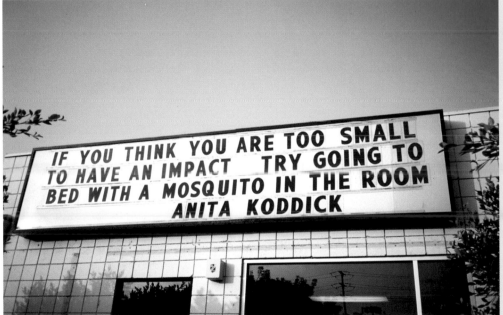

THE MARQUEE

As architects, we rarely have the opportunity to make broader cultural critiques in our day-to-day practice. Our second office had an existing marquee above the front windows. Rather than dismantling it, we thought the sign could be a good tool for communicating with our community. We posted a quotation on the marquee each week to engage strangers on the street in a dialogue on social and political issues. We tried to push the boundaries with the quotations that resonated within the context of Los Angeles, whether the link was direct or obtuse. For example, during the Los Angeles civil unrest in 1994, we put up a quotation from Martin Luther King, Jr., saying, "Riots are the language of the unheard." The marquee had a nearly religious following—if we were busy and missed a week, people would stop by and nag us to get something new up. For a while, we received more attention for our signs than for our architecture.

"In Los Angeles, you have to become fairly success-ful before you have a public voice. The sign was a way to quickly have a public voice—to just take it, get your ideas out there into the public forum, and see what happens. It was a weekly event that was sort of intellectually taxing, but mostly it was physi-cally taxing. To change the text, we used this long metal stick with a little rubber suction cup on the end. We had to wield this gigantic swordlike thing, smash it against the sign to suck the letters off, and put them back on.

"We went through maybe 300 quotes. The most controversial quote came from when Congress held the Meese Commission hearings on porno-graphy. It was so funny to hear these people talk about this report on pornography for hours and never admit that there could be something entertaining about porn. So Susie Bright, the pornography advocate, said something like, 'I masturbated to the Meese Commission report until I nearly passed out.' That quote caused quite a stir. We took it down when a client called and said that they drove by the sign with their kids, as they did every week, and now their children wanted to understand what the quote meant."
—*Anna Hill, Associate*

Guttentag Studio

EL NIÑO
"We were jamming into this hillside, throwing bearing piles for the foundation, with six feet of water. It was raining and pouring. There was plastic everywhere trying to keep the earth from eroding. We were soaking for days and weeks. Those were some of the tougher days. I can honestly say that I've literally been down in the trenches. I've gone from being in the trenches, to being a finish carpenter, to being a cabinet maker, to fabricating our modular homes."
—Hubert Plunkett, Construction Labor Staff

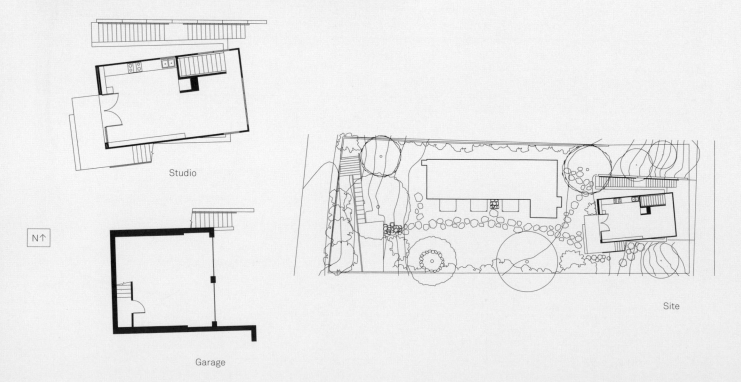

Studio

Garage

N↑

Site

Masonry construction

Exposed caissons

HILLSIDE CONSTRUCTION

We worked on the Guttentag Studio soon after the 1994 Northridge Earthquake, so we had to meet new, more stringent building codes. Sitting right in the hillside, the studio required major excavations and several deep caissons for structural support. Each caisson was forty feet deep. They looked ominous during construction before the rest of the building went up around them.

On top of all of that, we were building during Los Angeles's crazy El Niño year of endless rain and flooding, when Los Angeles had more precipitation than Seattle. The site also has underground streams, so water was constantly flowing. As soon as we dug the caissons, they filled up with water. We had to pour the concrete in the bottom of the hole and force the water out. Then we had to figure out ways to capture the dirty water that was forced from the holes. Unfortunately, the owner's cat disappeared around the time we were making those caissons for the foundation. We fear that the cat fell into the foundation holes and is somehow imbedded in the concrete now.

The Guttentag Studio was the first new building where Ron had free reign with the design. Though the budget was not high, the client, Mike Guttentag, gave us the freedom to explore in an open process. In the end, this became a very personal project, probably the most personal project until we worked on Ron's house, the Glencoe Residence, two years later.

Like many of the old cottages in the Santa Monica Canyons, Mike's home was originally constructed without a garage. The back of the property had a steep hill that cut down to an alley, so he commissioned us to design a new garage and a studio in this hillside. Ron created a design concept with two main volumes: an earthbound concrete block garage that sits perpendicular to the alley and a light, ethereal wood studio box that sits on top of the garage and opens onto the garden. One box rests gently on top of the other, as if simply placed there by a crane.

Setbacks and property lines dictated where the garage had to be located. The garage structure was designed to be very tall, stretching the height of the hillside, in order to act as a foundation for the studio. If the studio box was aligned perfectly with the garage, it would have peered directly into the main house. Instead, we made the upper volume slightly askew so that the studio looks down the length of the backyard to create a sense of one continuous indoor-outdoor space, helping to break down the mass, and separate the studio from the box below. This simple idea of one box sitting on another has become a basic principle in our designs. Many projects since this studio—from the Ward Luu Residence to our new pre-fabs—come from this one small project.

CLIENT INVOLVEMENT

"I didn't have a lot of money to spend at the time, so I was thinking about doing some of the construction work myself. I saw real appeal in working with a firm that was open to a client who wants to enter not just into the design process but into the construction process as well. I did the landscaping and the fencing myself, and they took care of everything else. At one point, my cousin and I did the hardwood floors, and understandably, Ron insisted that we tear them out and have his people do it. Generally, any of the construction within the building that I did was rejected and had to be redone.

"I've always been interested in the construction process. Several years after my studio was complete, I convinced Ron and Leo to hire me as a laborer for $10 an hour. I was a helper in the metal shop with Scott Enge. I did metal cutting, grinding, patina finishes. I worked on all of those windows at the Hilltop Studio. At first, being on my feet and moving things around the shop was so tiring. I loved it so much, but I got a job as a visiting professor of law and had to take that opportunity."
—*Mike Guttentag, Client*

Keeping with the essential aspects of the boxes, the materials in the project are very simple, basic, and raw. The garage volume is made with exposed, standard concrete-masonry block, while the studio volume is clad in natural wood siding that we left to age. Both boxes use unadorned steel doors and windows. In contrast, the interiors are maple and look very polished. Like an oyster, the project has a rough exterior and a smooth, protected interior.

We integrated a roof terrace into the top of the studio volume. When we designed the building, we planned the terrace to provide views to the surrounding canyons. Once we completed the rough framing in construction, we all climbed up on a ladder and saw the ocean for the first time from the property.

View into studio with stairs up to roof terrace at right

Kaufmann House Restoration

"Because I had been around architects and architecture long enough, I knew the restoration wasn't going to be a project that was going to be directed by a contactor, so we immediately went to preservation architecture firms. To be honest, nobody wanted to do it. It was very frustrating. We were dragging people to look at the project. David Gebhard, the architectural historian up in Santa Barbara, gave me advice to 'just find someone who can fix a house that has a lot of metal and steel.' My friend at school worked for Frank Gehry, whose work Ron and Leo restored. He said, 'There are these guys who've done some work repairing our complex homes. I think they would really have a good appreciation for the building.' That was it—I called them up, and they fell all over the project.

"We had to go by our gut, and the overwhelming thing for us was that they really, really, really liked the building. I felt that they understood the architect well, and they were willing to share the project with us. Design-build was also a factor. There are so many things that have to go into building. We wanted to have architects who enjoyed the building process. And we also felt that doing modern architecture is a lot about constructing space and the use of materials. Without ornamentation, building something that is very minimalist is the most difficult thing in the world to do, so we knew we were going to have to have real craftspeople. Our thought was that if they are this passionate, they will find the right people."
—*Beth Harris, Client*

We were working in our office one summer day in 1992 when the phone rang, and Ron picked up. "Hi. This is Beth Harris," the voice said. "We've just purchased the Kaufmann House in Palm Springs and would like to speak to you about doing the restoration." We were excited simply to have the opportunity to see the house, let alone get to do any work on it. On a blistering hot day, soon after the phone call from Beth, we went out to see the house and could feel the presence and the power of Richard Neutra's original 1946 design. However, we were also pained by the current condition of the home. After the Kaufmanns sold the house, subsequent owners transformed the home into a year-round residence. They made significant alterations and additions to the house, removing many of the original finishes and nearly doubling the size of the original home. We were thrilled to restore the Kaufmann House but also knew that, working with a building of such cultural importance, it would be difficult to both design and construct.

The restoration process began by establishing the program and methodology. Beth, who was getting a doctorate in architectural history at the time, took the lead in developing a rigorous restoration philosophy for returning the home to the original form, size, and materiality, as shown in Julius Shulman's famous twilight photograph from 1947. This meant retaining as much of the original material as possible and removing the subsequent additions. In places where no historic material remained, we used both archival and on-site archeological research to determine the original products and construction methods that Neutra used. For every original building component that was still in the home, we first tried to clean the material to bring it up to usable condition. If that was insufficient, we then tried repairing the material, and if all else failed, our last resort was replacing the material.

Construction on the Kaufmann House

ESTABLISHING THE RESTORATION PHILOSOPHY

"At the very beginning of the process, David Gebhard, the historian at University of California Santa Barbara, gave me very good advice. He said, 'Decide what it is that you want to try to do, and then write it down. I don't know Ron and Leo, and I don't know you and Brent all that well, but if you have something to guide you, you can always amend it.' He made a good case that there would be so many times when we would have to make decisions about if we wanted to take the time or allow the expense to do something a particular way. And so we had decided very early on to go back to the 1946 condition.

"From the very beginning, we went into the project looking at the house not as a piece of real estate but as a work of art. It just felt like we should see how the house was when it was at its best, to see if we could begin to understand, conceptually, what Neutra was trying to do in the original design. The Kaufmann House was one of the few buildings where Neutra got to do almost everything he wanted since he had a very agreeable client with all the money in the world. I just always felt, since the first time I saw the house in print, that it was probably one of the great modern masterpieces."
—Beth Harris, Client

We regularly conferred with Beth and Brent Harris in long, challenging meetings to discuss the various options at hand. They wanted to know all the options and to make the best possible decision for the house—not for us, not for them, but for the house. They were extremely consistent and disciplined. Ultimately, all of the decisions came back to the original restoration philosophy.

To research the original materials and details, Chris Shanley, the architectural project manager, and many others spent nearly four months in the archives at the University of California Los Angeles that hold Neutra's original papers. Since photocopies were not allowed, our staff redrew, by hand, every single drawing and documented all of the specifications and correspondence that they found. Beyond the archive's holdings, we found many of the best sources in the house itself, uncovering swatches of original material that we could then analyze and replicate in areas where the historic fabric was no longer available. As the general contractors, we had the control we needed to carry out such careful archaeology.

Looking at actual fixtures or original specifications, we identified what products Neutra used and developed a methodology for sourcing materials or fabricating replications. While Neutra used many off-the-shelf products, often those materials were no longer in production and now

Julius Shulman and Fordyce "Red" Marsh

The restoration provided the wonderful opportunity to meet with many people who helped shape mid-century modern architeture. We learned so much from talking to the architects Albert Frey and Philip Johnson, the photographer Julius Shulman, and the contractor Fordyce "Red" Marsh. Everyone was so supportive and excited that we took the time to talk to them, and since they were always older than us, there was a great sense of elders passing down information. Several of the meetings were very emotional. After we visited Red Marsh's house, his wife pulled us aside and told us how much she appreciated our talking to Red because no one ever asked him about his time working with Neutra. These interactions gave us personal connections to the history of the site as well as a greater appreciation for their truly forward-thinking work.

"Red Marsh had a very personal relationship with Neutra, acting as the builder on many of his buildings, so we visited him at his house. We talked to him about building Neutra's homes so we could understand Neutra's intent from drawings to execution. This was as close as possible to getting into the mind of Neutra, to getting his perspective on executing details.

"Red taught us that Neutra was always pushing the technology and construction capabilities, trying to make things perfect. One big question during the restoration was whether we should upgrade the quality of the construction to today's standards. When we could upgrade the construction without any visual impact, we would for the sake of longevity. However, if a new technique would be visual, we deferred to the 1947 appearance. For example, the craftsmanship of the drawer pull was quite clumsy and not integrated into the main front of the cabinet. In the end, we replicated the clumsier casework detail. Even if Neutra could have used the more sophisticated detail, he didn't use it at Kaufmann. The cabinet maker, Kurt Gary, kept Shulman's photos in his shop to find veneer that matched. It would take weeks to get the right veneer. He would call and say, 'I think I have a match!'"
—*Chris Shanley, Architectural Project Manager*

Julius Shulman with his iconic twilight photo

JULIUS SHULMAN

We would be hard-pressed to overstate the importance of Julius Shulman's role in the restoration of the Kaufmann House. Beyond our conversations with Julius, his photographs guided us throughout the project. During construction, we kept one set of his photos on the site and one set in our office so we could discuss information with the site, both looking at the photos.

"Neutra created a house which he thought should echo the most important element that any architect can pursue—that this would be a desert house that would attend to all of the qualities that you could attribute to living in a home in the desert. Unfortunately, during the ensuing years after the Kaufmanns left, the house was sold and resold and sold and resold, and every successive resident took a chunk out of the body of the house. Finally, when the Harrises acquired the house, it was literally in a state of destruction.

"Along come Leo, Ron, and the Harrises, who knew I had tremendous coverage of the house from the photography I did with Neutra. There is no time element in my mind. We went several times to every one of Neutra's early houses, which is what accounts for the presence in my files of so many photographs. At my house one weekend, Beth and Brent were here. I pulled out of my files this huge box of prints, several hundred 8x10 glossy prints. Then ensued a grab bag kind of thing. They didn't know where to start. When they saw my photographs, the Harrises looked at each other—'Look, it's all in front of us.' Marmol has said publicly that the house couldn't have been restored without my photographs."
—*Julius Shulman, Photographer*

required custom fabrication. We talked to original fabricators and suppliers around the world to determine what options were available. We ended up sourcing glass from Scotland, cork tiles from Portugal. We scavenged the United States for salvaged vintage plumbing fixtures, refabricated lighting fixtures Neutra originally designed for the home, and found the one metal shop in the country that had the right dies to produce sheet metal that matched the original. Chris even convinced a quarry in Utah to open up an old excavation site to source the Utah Buff Sandstone from the same stone that Neutra used fifty years earlier.

We only made slight deviations from the home's original condition for the sake of improving the longevity of the house, such as integrating new structural upgrades or adding sophisticated heating and cooling systems. To maintain the original design integrity, we went to great lengths to hide the upgrades from view. For example, we designed the HVAC system to distribute air through toe spaces in the cabinets, linear diffusers, and other hidden methods.

All in all, we spent nearly five years working on the Kaufmann House. In the process, we met mid-century legends, architectural scholars, and gifted craftspeople who endured long meetings, desert summer heat, and obsessive attention to detail to help us revive this icon of Modernism.

Uncovered original writing

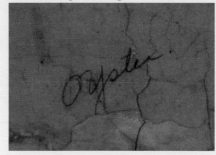

RESTORATION AS ARCHEOLOGY

"The house was like an archeological dig where you slowly remove layers to get to the original material, even just to get a small section of an original paint color. We uncovered handwritten construction notes on the plaster that read 'Oyster' and 'Canary Yellow' as direction for the original painters for the correct wall color. These were incredibly intimate moments. We would get phone calls from the site when they would find something wonderful. Like one day they found an old toilet, possibly from the original house, literally buried somewhere in a boulder field on the grounds. I kept hoping to find a buried set of plans since the UCLA archive had no working drawings or construction drawings, possibly because Neutra's office suffered a fire in the sixties."
—*Chris Shanley, Architectural Project Manager*

MATCHING THE MICA

Original specifications for the house mention a mica plaster finish, but the house had been painted so many times, there were no remnants of the original finish. During the removal of one of the additions to the house, we carefully took down a bathroom near the staff wing. In that bathroom, there was a small electrical box, maybe six inches by three inches in area, that we removed from one of the original walls. Miraculously, the small area of wall behind the box had never been painted, so there we saw the original, glistening mica finish. This was the only area in the entire house where we found the finish. Mica is only extracted by a few remaining mines in the country, so we contacted the United States Bureau of Mines to get information on those companies. We matched the samples sent by those mines with the small area on the original wall to determine the best source for the new mica finish.

FIREPLACE MASONRY

"The fireplace was a block shell that had been veneered, and it was leaking very badly. These days, we use galvanized nails or screws in masonry, but back then the materials weren't galvanized. A lot of nails and ties had rusted. It was a big project to restore. The architects didn't want us to take off any more stonework than was necessary, so we couldn't start at the top of the chimney and move down to the deck. Instead, we started down about five or six feet from the top, took out part of the stones, put shores in to keep the remaining pieces from collapsing, and then removed the stone down to the deck. That was a lot of work. With the existing stone work, we took pictures and made drawings. As the stones were removed, we tagged and numbered them so that they would go back just the way they were originally. It was a lot slower, a lot more detailed than the normal stone jobs we do."
—*Clive Christie, Mason*

Fireplace masonry shoring

View of the "gloriette," an open-air, rooftop deck

MATCHING THE ORIGINAL FASCIA SHEET METAL

Nobody wants a leaky roof, particularly over a masterpiece of modern architecture, so we place great importance on waterproofing. Carefully detailed and fabricated flashing, essentially shielding made from sheet metal, is critical to weatherproofing because it covers and protects joints and edges. From our own sheet metal shop, we know the challenges of considering all of the unique conditions that require protection and the skilled fabrication necessary to prevent leaks.

At the Kaufmann House, we found that much of the original fascia sheet metal was too rusty and required replacement. Patching all over the roof clearly showed that this waterproofing system failed long ago. We carefully removed all of the sheet metal to determine which pieces were in good enough condition to protect the house over the coming years. With 85 percent of the metal, if we chose to reuse it, we would be accepting the fact that the house would leak. We decided that the longevity of the house outweighed the importance of retaining this decayed historic fabric.

To recreate the crimped sheet metal, we sent samples of the original material to forty metal shops across the country. One of them had old machinery in the corner of their shop, so they experimented to match the color, pattern, and texture of the sample. In an old catalog of dies, they found a stamp that produced the correct pattern. The Harrises paid to have the die repaired. However, that die still had a bald spot that left one part of the metal "under-crimped," so they had to increase the pressure, "over crimp" the metal, and then press out eight one-thousandths of an inch to make the crimp consistently the same depth as the original.

Sheet metal installation

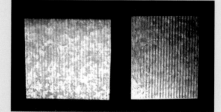

Historic sample on left; recreation on right

38

THE WHITE CONCRETE TOPPING SLAB

"In looking at Shulman's photos, we realized there were no control joints in the concrete from the entry through the living room, dining area, hallway, gallery, and master bedroom. That meant between 1,200 and 1,800 square feet of concrete had to be placed all at once. The concrete subcontractor was very nervous because he hadn't done a project of that scale with this type of concrete. The rich mixture of concrete and sand was slushy and could not be pumped, so they had to wheelbarrow the concrete by hand and dump it one wheelbarrow at a time. We built a three-quarter scale mock-up of the entire area, complete with partial height walls, in an empty adjacent lot so the concrete subcontractor could figure out how to work the pour. Since the concrete was white, we were very worried about tracking in mud. With concrete, you only get one try. There was just so much at stake, so we had to get it right. On the day of the pour, we put down plywood, created a path for the concrete to be wheelbarrowed into the house, and hosed down the boots of the guys each time they came inside. It was a large crew, about twenty-five guys, with six of them just wheelbarrowing and the rest finishing the concrete, which needs to be worked quickly. It took about eight hours to get the slab set before we could begin the finishing work. We worked from 6a.m. until 10 at night."
—Chris Shanley, *Architectural Project Manager*

INTEGRATING NEW SYSTEMS

Many of the walls in the house no longer provided structural support because so much duct work had been placed in them. To provide for protection against future earthquakes, we needed to find new ways to support the structure. We worked with the structural engineer to conceal lateral bracing and moment-resistant steel columns in the walls and thick roof sections. We knew a functioning HVAC system was essential both to make the home habitable year-round and to protect the materials in the home from deterioration due to extreme temperature swings in the desert. We did not want to run the ductwork through a dropped ceiling, which would alter Neutra's ceiling height, nor did we want to run the ductwork outside, which would ruin the original roofline. We chose to put the HVAC duct work underground since we needed to replace much of the original topping slab anyway. Sections of the original floor had been damaged over time by coverings like carpet, so we placed new ducts in those sections and worked around the preserved historic material.

LANDSCAPE

Julius Shulman's early photographs show the house floating in the desert, with boulder fields and creosote bush in the distance beyond an oleander hedge. Now suburban homes surround the Kaufmann House, infringing on the original expansive experience of the home's interaction with the landscape. Because of these close neighbors, in the restoration we had to bring the desert landscape closer to the house than it had been originally while still trying to create as much visual depth as possible with the design. Like backdrops on a stage, we tried to design the landscape to appear deeper than it really was. We carefully planned the layers of plantings to create landscaped screens that defined where there was transparency, and where there was opacity. Neutra called the Kaufmann House a "ship on the desert." We wanted to make the desert feel as natural as possible.

"Bill Matthews and I were the site supervisors on the Kaufmann House restoration. I lived on-site in the old pool house five nights a week for almost three years. The house had such a manufactured feel, like a machine that just sits on the landscape. We thought the landscape should be less structured and not too formalized, so there would be no competition between the two entities.

"We saw what was native to the area and how it changed with the seasons. We did research into growers in Anza Borrego, Yucca Valley, Arizona, and other desert areas to find natural desert plants. Along the perimeter of the site, we added California Fan Palms, which are found in natural oases in the desert, to screen adjacent properties. The way the palms grow naturally, the old leaves hang down against the trunk and built-up thatch. There can be fifteen- or twenty-year-old leaves on the tree, so it shows different life cycles. When they delivered the palms, we asked them to leave the old dead leaves on the plant to build up more mass. We also embellished existing boulder piles and created new boulder piles throughout the landscape. We brought in additional rocks and also used large granite boulders that we unearthed during trenching for the HVAC system in the house."
—Eric Lamers, Site Supervisor

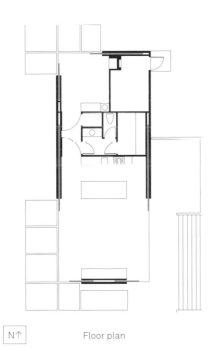

Floor plan

The Harrises wanted to use the Kaufmann House as a year-round vacation home, but the restoration philosophy of returning the home to Richard Neutra's 1946 design did not allow for the integration of the modern amenities typical of a luxury vacation home. While we felt comfortable invisibly integrating new structural systems into the Kaufmann House, there was no way we would integrate something like a steam room into Neutra's structure. The Harrises decided they wanted a pool house that could act as a receptacle for the contemporary conveniences of a full-size kitchen, advanced audio-visual equipment, exercise room, and steam room. This decision meant that we faced the terrifying task of creating a new building in close proximity to Neutra's masterpiece.

We decided early on that the pool house should not try to mimic the Kaufmann House and instead should sit as background on the site. The pool house had to separate itself by character, not by distance. Ron wanted to respect the proportions of the Neutra building, but if someone came on site, he wanted them to know immediately that the pool house was not part of the original Neutra design. The new building became earthier to be a part of the landscape. Whereas the Kaufmann House has brilliant white concrete floors, the pool house concrete contains brown pigmentation. Similarly, a shimmering mica glaze covered many of the exterior walls at the Kaufmann House, so at the pool house we selected plaster with a very deep green tone.

DEMATERIALIZING THE BUILDING

"You think that designing a simple building to be as transparent as possible should be simple, but it is incredibly difficult. Two sides of the pool house have essentially sliding, mechanized glass walls for half the facade. They are so big—nineteen feet wide—that I wouldn't even call them doors. This is the modern sliding door on steroids; I think Neutra would have loved the opportunity to use them.

"When you are inside the pool house and look out at the Kaufmann House, the pool house feels like it disappears and becomes only air. The perforated shade awning helps dematerialize the building, too. You barely even notice the awning from a distance and just see a small, four-inch fascia. The color palette of the pool house allows the building to recede so the landscaping fills in the space around it. We spent a lot of time trying to keep the whole pool house within an appropriate scale while still maximizing the ceiling height. We wanted the proportion on the outside to match the feel of the space inside, so we designed a narrow two-inch parapet on the roof that required special approval from the roofing manufacturer."
—*Chris Shanley, Architectural Project Manager*

Since solid-roof overhangs help define the machine aesthetic of the Kaufmann House, we thought that solid overhangs at the pool house would read too much as a replication of Neutra's design. We wanted the new house to feel lighter, and instead designed cantilevers made from two layers of stainless-steel mesh. Exposed steel I beams support the wide cantilevers while the sky shines through the holes in the mesh. When the sun shines through, the lacy steel mesh makes an intricate moiré shadow pattern on the ground.

True to Neutra's spirit, we used large cantilevers, wide glass openings, and open corners to make the pool house feel expansive, connect to the outdoors, and provide views back to the Kaufmann House. Even though the pool house is fairly small, these design choices made for a very complex structural system. Pocketing doors and recessed shade pockets require voids in the walls and ceilings to hide the doors and shades from sight. Yet those voids leave little room to insert the structural supports for the building. We spent a lot of time working with a structural engineer to achieve a building that had the right proportions and attributes while at the same time met the building code.

We understand that at a very basic level, the pool house probably should not be there, certainly not so close to Neutra's work. But we also understand the client's desire to have a pool house and to have that pool house located next to the pool. So we used these elements of earthy materials, lacy overhangs, and open structural systems to create a respectful yet distinctive building. The pool house is an insertion, and it clearly reads as one.

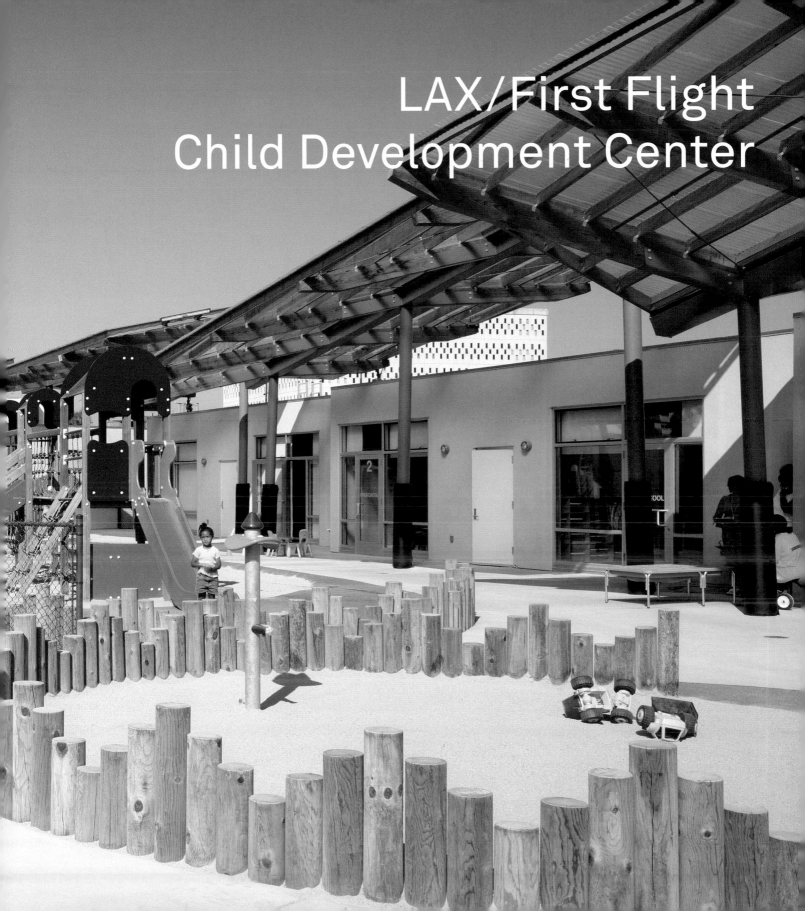

LAX/First Flight
Child Development Center

Child's drawing of airport imagery

EDUCATIONAL PHILOSOPHIES
Since this was our first child care project, we worked closely with an educational consultant, Mary Hartzell, to understand the best environments for fostering early childhood development. Through these consultations, we settled on an approach that was about smaller spaces, scaled to children, with teachers and caretakers staffed appropriately to handle smaller groups. The airport authority's educational consultant agreed with this fundamental philosophy that smaller spaces create a better, more intimate educational environment. While the smaller spaces no doubt required more vigilant supervision, we believed the higher burden placed on the childcare provider was a worthwhile tradeoff for the educational benefits of intimately scaled spaces.

The LAX/First Flight Child Development Center was a turning point for the office. We were still a young firm when we entered the public competition to design a childcare center for the children of the Los Angeles International Airport's employees. We knew the only chance we had at landing this job was to throw ourselves into a broad and rigorous competition entry. At that point, none of us had any children or experience with child care projects. We spent a tremendous amount of time talking with the client, reviewing the request for proposals, and researching child care to understand the project and put together a comprehensive competition entry.

As we looked at children's drawings about airplanes and airports, we found it hard not to see wings at every turn. We took that imagery and abstracted it. We didn't want to do this in a literal way, so we created

COMPETITIONS

"I think competitions are eighty percent research and communicating your ability to do rigorous work, and twenty percent design. Once you actually win the project, the design idea is revised twenty times anyway, so you just want to demonstrate your ability to intuit who they are and what they need. In a competition situation, we want to understand our client backward and forward, and we want to put together the ideal team of consultants for that particular client. We've always had this same philosophy about competitions—that it's only worth pursuing if you really intend to win. If we're going to go after a competition, we want to give one hundred and ten percent because it is so costly to lose."
—*Anna Hill, Associate*

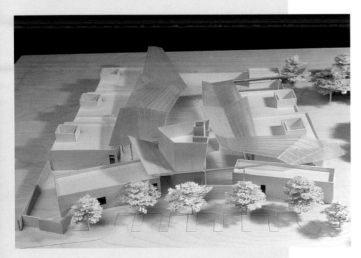

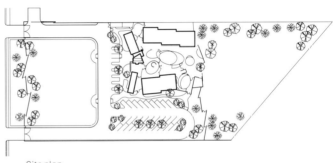

Site plan

N↑

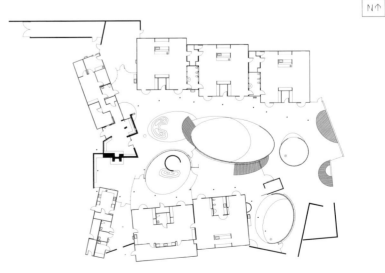

Floor plan

Foundation before module delivery

Wood sheer-wall prefab modules

PREFAB

LAX/First Flight Child Development Center was our first experience using prefabricated modular structures. The airport's master plan was in flux as we started this project, so they asked that the child care center be "moveable" if the master plan changed in the future. To meet this requirement, we turned to wood, sheer-wall modular structures to create the backbone of the design. The classroom modules are simple wood boxes that compose the majority of the square-footage of the project. We spent a lot of time investigating how we could turn modular construction into a warm environment with natural materials.

Since the primary buildings were prefabricated while the entry tower and shade structures were site built, it became a challenge to integrate the site-built with the modular. This was particularly difficult on a tight budget and with only six months for construction. The reality is that the buildings could not be moved easily, but for us it became a valuable opportunity to learn about prefabrication in a traditional context.

Canopy construction

shade canopies that evoke airplane wings, and the entry tower is reminiscent of flight control towers. At LAX—and later at the TBWA\Chiat\Day offices—the design is not a replica of the narratives, but rather we used the theme as a device to arrive at the formal design.

Surrounded by four acres of park, the center incorporates classrooms, administrative offices, staff facilities, and a large outdoor play area. Since an integral part of child care is about security and protection, we laid out the buildings around an inner courtyard. The buildings form a simple U-shape that opens up to the park behind the site. Classrooms have exposed wood ceilings and wide expanses of glass that face the central play yard to fill the spaces with natural light. We kept the buildings as simple as possible and then put the real complexity into the shade canopies.

We used translucent shade canopies to provide protection from the rain and sun as well as to create a distinctive, uplifting quality to the space. The columns for the canopies tilt in a playful way to create an informal environment that is contemporary without being rigidly orthogonal. One day, during the on-site inspection of the steel, the inspector pulled the site supervisor aside and said, "You know, none of the columns are plumb. Nothing is straight."

As we look back at the center, each now with children of our own, we appreciate the final design even more—the intimate scale, the integration of indoor and outdoor spaces, and the overall upbeat environment.

DESIGNING FOR KIDS

"When you start talking about kids, everybody puts in their two cents. For example, neighbors said our color selections were 'too sophisticated' for the kids, meaning that they weren't primary colors. But all of the consultants and education providers that we talked to were telling us that primary colors were too much for kids. They agreed that the building should be the backdrop to the educational classes and not so bold and distracting. I mean, kids need to nap in these spaces."
—*Nicole Starr, Architectural Project Manager*

Costume National

True to Los Angeles' annual calendar, the Costume National store was timed to open a week before the Academy Awards. That meant our staff had three months to design and construct the space. The clients were in Milan most of the time, and once we showed them renderings of the space, they just said, "Go!" For the clients, time was more important than budget, so we had to make quick decisions and figure out the rest as we went along. As the general contractor for the project, we had significant design influence on site. The extent to which we were able to work through details during the construction was a true testament to the power of design-build. There are a lot of things that, looking back, we could have done more intelligently. But that is OK; there is something refreshing about not having the time to overthink things. In the end, we pulled it all together for the opening party, where we strolled through the store in our new gifts, Costume National clothes.

Costume National is very much an urban brand, and their clothing is all about the city. When the Milan fashion house approached us to work on a 3,000-square-foot store in Los Angeles, they wanted a space that captured the light and attitude of our city. While their store in New York is completely black, on this project they wanted a space that was much brighter. We brought Los Angeles, with all of its light and attitude, into the store by playing with the natural and artificial, with desire and sexiness, with openness and nuance.

From the beginning, the owners of Costume National wanted a white store. For them, it seemed more urban, more L.A. We took that direction and introduced different shades of white, gray, taupe, and gold. The main clothing displays incorporate smooth white lacquered panels floating off the structural walls with concealed lighting behind. We carried over some ideas from the New York store to create a consistent aesthetic. For example, the New York store used fiber-optic lighting, so we expanded on that idea and used fiber-optic lights to outline the shelves and create halos around the hanging areas. This backlit effect gives an ethereal glow to the clothes and holds them up as prized objects. We created a gallerylike presentation for

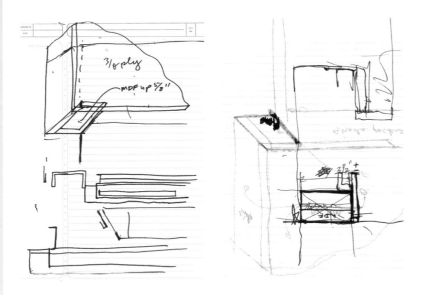

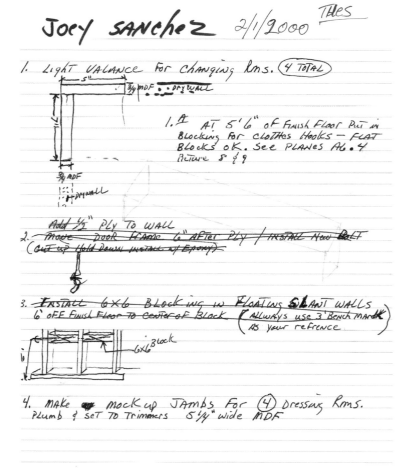

"The whole project was so fast. We came up with the concept with the clients on site then did the drawings very quickly. On projects with that speed, you have to develop things that can be built quickly. You got to a certain point when you need to just start building and finish the rest as you go along. I was sketching out the detail drawings physically on the dry wall. Toward the end, there was so much going on, and going on so fast, that I was onsite everyday. Those last few weeks were such a blur. I remember going to the glamorous opening party, but I don't really remember much more than that since I was so stressed. At the same time, these projects have instant gratification as opposed to a house, which seems to take forever."
—Stephanie Hobbs, *Architectural Project Manager*

Site meeting notes and sketches

VOYEURISM AND SHOPPING

We used neutral colors, open spaces, and light to create a gallerylike environment that holds up the clothes as art objects. Traditionally, retail stores have street-front windows filled with mannequins modeling the clothes in a staged window display. However, at Costume National the windows open onto the actual shopping environment, so you can catch a glimpse of sexy people shopping for sexy clothes. This voyeuristic, erotic environment of fashion parallels the sexy playfulness of the space. It's a theater of high design. The idea is to celebrate this natural voyeurism since there's something fundamentally human in this playful sexiness.

THE STEEL SCREEN: RENDERING VS. REALITY

"Costume National's clothing uses materials that are iridescent and see-through, so we designed a backdrop at the far end of the store that was like a stainless steel veil you could see through. In our renderings, the screen looked perfect and smooth—very ethereal. But once it was fabricated, the metal was too raw. You could feel too much of the reality of the material. The clients came in for a final site walk-through, just three days before their opening Oscar party. They immediately didn't like the screen when they saw it. It was just too heavy. The metal was so dark, so extreme— it looked bad. The project manager, Steph, and I still don't agree on this. Luckily, since we were the contractors, we took it down and made it work in time for the party."
—Ron

"On a computer, the metal screen probably looked good. It was a big grid, so it looked fairly clean and straight. The screen was basically a two-dimensional object, like a giant piece of paper that went all over. It didn't have three-dimensional depth, which in reality made it very difficult to make the screen appear to be flat and true. The screen was very large, maybe fourteen feet tall, so it had to be pieced together out of parts. That created problems with screw joints and getting even tension across the entire screen. Essentially, the design surpassed the material tolerance. It was a geometric idea that had some rationale, but it wasn't buildable in the space, in the time, and with the materials we had."
—Scott Enge, Metal Shop Manager

Costume National's famous shoes by sparsely displaying them on floor-to-ceiling Lucite® shelves backlit by fiber-optic lighting as well. To add nuance to the palette we created oval-shaped suede and leather seating in light brown and gold.

In Los Angeles, we're designing for people driving by at thirty miles per hour, so we need to engage them quickly from the street. One of our first design decisions was to enlarge the six display windows of the former restaurant space to be nearly floor-to-ceiling height, providing an immediate connection to the street. To emphasize the allure of the bright, white interior spaces, we selected a dark shade of warm gray to paint the exterior of the store, creating a contrast that allowed the windows to glow and create intrigue.

Inside the store, capturing and exploring the variations of natural and artificial light became one of our primary focuses. Natural light floods the space through the large windows and elongated skylights. Because the store is a sampling of light hues, with different levels of gloss, at times the subtle variations play tricks on your eyes. A wall can appear to be one color in different light or different colors in the same light, making interactions of shadow and translucency.

TBWA\Chiat\Day
San Francisco Offices

"I wrote a book about the mid-century architect Albert Frey, so I was very aware of the Kaufmann House restoration. Then I befriended the owners of the Rustic Canyon Residence. When I walked into their clapboard home that the firm designed and built in their early years, it was so well thought out and comfortable. Even though it was a more traditional style, I really wanted to replicate the psychological space of that house.

"Establishing this new office begged the question of what's unique to San Francisco, what should a Chiat Day San Francisco office feel and look like, and how do we differentiate ourselves from the mothership. I was looking for an architecture firm that was emerging, not established. My CFO said, 'Someone had finally figured out the size of cubes and how many people you can fit into X cubic feet, so why would we work with a company that has never done this before?' And that was a very fair question. I needed the right people to win that argument.

"I had this recognition when I met this team that they were so responsive and really listened. It's a cliché, but they lacked that architectural arrogance. They cared about us, how we worked, how we functioned as a team, and how we functioned as a culture. What was really impressive about Leo, Ron, and Anna Hill, the project manager, was that they not only had the talent and sensibility, but they also had the depth of team. We're very aware in our business of who in the team will really produce the project. We were very impressed that as emerging as they were, structurally, the company had Ron's design talent, Leo's business skills and management acumen, and Anna's intelligent and thoughtful approach. Ultimately, the process was impeccable. Our CFO is a very rigorous man, and at the end of the day, he said of all of the construction he'd been through, this was exceptional."
—*Jennifer Golub, Client*

Instead of designing in a narrative-driven approach, we usually prefer to work with the abstract ideas about space and form—the key elements of material, proportion, and quality of space. But with TBWA\Chiat\Day's San Francisco office, we were designing spaces for an advertising agency whose very work is to build brands and stories for their clients. In their own history, Chiat Day's offices have used architecture to define their identity. Given the nature of advertising and Chiat Day's architectural history, we tried to use what was unique about the office's culture and site to create a narrative and identity for the space.

We set out to learn about the client, the city, and the site itself. We spent several days in San Francisco, walking around, visiting the history museums and local monuments. As we were looking for unique attributes that could inform our design, we uncovered the wild history that lay beneath Chiat Day's building. One hundred and fifty years earlier, the building's site was part of the city's teaming port when sea captains, stricken with Gold Rush fever, abandoned their ships at shore and headed for the hills in search of gold. Over time, the harbor was filled in to create buildable land, leaving the 49ers' ships embedded in the new ground. Once we realized that 55 Union Street was sitting on reclaimed land, with buried ships under the foundation, we knew we had found our narrative.

We developed the story of a storm that flooded the entire building, washing objects from the foundation's past into the new space. In the narrative, the force of the water tore holes in the floor plates and entangled

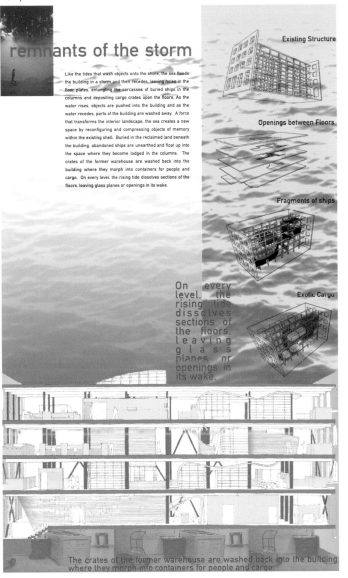

remnants of the storm

Like the tides that wash objects onto the shore, the sea floods the building in a storm and then recedes, leaving holes in the floor plates, entangling the carcasses of buried ships in the columns and depositing cargo crates upon the floors. As the water rises, objects are pushed into the building and as the water recedes, parts of the building are washed away. A force that transforms the interior landscape, the sea creates a new space by reconfiguring and compressing objects of memory within the existing shell. Buried in the reclaimed land beneath the building, abandoned ships are unearthed and float up into the space where they become lodged in the columns. The crates of the former warehouse are washed back into the building where they morph into containers for people and cargo. On every level, the rising tide dissolves sections of the floors, leaving glass planes or openings in its wake.

Existing Structure

Openings between Floors

Fragments of ships

Exotic Cargo

On every level, the rising tide dissolves sections of the floors, leaving glass planes or openings in its wake.

The crates of the former warehouse are washed back into the building where they morph into containers for people and cargo.

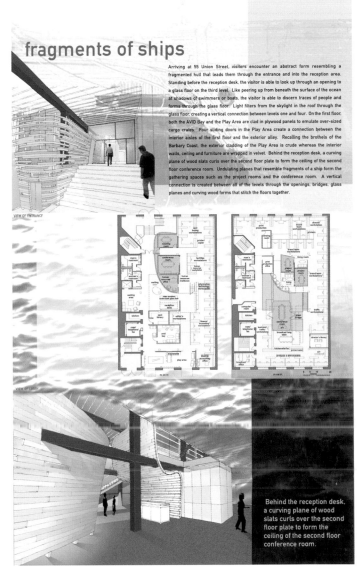

fragments of ships

Arriving at 55 Union Street, visitors encounter an abstract form resembling a fragmented hull that leads them through the entrance and into the reception area. Standing before the reception desk, the visitor is able to look up through an opening to a glass floor on the third level. Like peering up from beneath the surface of the ocean at shadows of swimmers or boats, the visitor is able to discern traces of people and forms through the glass floor. Light filters from the skylight in the roof through the glass floor, creating a vertical connection between levels one and four. On the first floor, both the AVID Bay and the Play Area are clad in plywood panels to emulate over-sized cargo crates. Four sliding doors in the Play Area create a connection between the interior aisles of the first floor and the exterior alley. Recalling the brothels of the Barbary Coast, the exterior cladding of the Play Area is crude whereas the interior walls, ceiling and furniture are wrapped in velvet. Behind the reception desk, a curving plane of wood slats curls over the second floor plate to form the ceiling of the second floor conference room. Undulating planes that resemble fragments of a ship form the gathering spaces such as the project rooms and the conference room. A vertical connection is created between all of the levels through the openings, bridges, glass planes and curving wood forms that stitch the floors together.

VIEW OF ENTRANCE

VIEW OF LOBBY

Behind the reception desk, a curving plane of wood slats curls over the second floor plate to form the ceiling of the second floor conference room.

"Anna Hill, the project manager, did the most thorough and thoughtful inquiry, learning our business and working with every department. She really got it and understood the work of the various disciplines. She and I toured probably fifteen different editorial spaces so she could experience different types of edit bays, and the size, sounds, and different types of ventilation. We have a very densely packed program, and every inch functions beautifully. I get to enjoy that every day."
—*Jennifer Golub, Client*

FURNITURE

Working with the water archaeology theme, we initially had two concepts for the furniture: a crate motif and sea creature motif that included a biomorphic, seventies palette. Over time, the sea life theme gradually shifted to become boxier, but we never lost interest in the color.

"We developed the full furniture plan for the office, including specifying furniture and designing some custom pieces. We designed five tables inspired by Gerrit Rietvelt's crate furniture, which was modular. We carried that idea across and designed tables made from plywood that are simple, boxy, and low with interesting voids in them. We designed two huge conference tables that were so large they had to be assembled in the conference room. We did not do a lot of prototyping, but since the smaller pieces were done in our cabinet shop, I was able to check up on them during production. We were always interested in pushing furniture as low as it can go. We liked that it created a bit of self-consciousness for the clients."
—*Michael Ned Holte, Furniture Designer*

ship carcasses in the building's frame. This conceptual palette of abandoned ships, crates, and materials provided the point of departure for the design. To create a strong sense of entry for visitors and employees, we used bowing architectural forms that abstractly refer to these buried ships. Chiat Day flourishes in collaborative work environments, so we made informal "living room" areas and opened up the floor plate to establish visual connections between various departments.

The maritime concept also allowed us to explore materials that brought warmth into the building. In the context of foggy San Francisco, the staff at Chiat Day told us that creating a comfortable, home-like environment was essential for sustaining their long work days. We started by stripping down the building to the existing brick walls, wood ceilings, timber columns, and large glass windows. Playing off those textures, we selected seagrass mats, cork, and plywood as the primary flooring materials. For the main forms, we used plywood wall panels and workstations, tackable burlap wall panels, Douglas Fir planking, and steel cable railing systems. We also filled the offices with natural light by virtually eliminating all interior walls and using translucent polycarbonate walls to refract light and obscure forms as a visual allusion to water.

This project had the potential to be very difficult during construction, given our distance from San Francisco and the inherent challenges of working within an existing structure. Luckily, the project went so smoothly, thanks to the excellent local contractor, CIC Associates, and the visionary client we had in Chiat Day.

THE CUBE

"For the work spaces, we used the metaphor of 'a crate for living and working.' In designing the cube, we saw that subtle moves have a huge effect. The height made a big difference in regards to privacy and exposure. While people were sitting, we wanted them to have some sense of enclosure but also to be able to see people who walked by. We ended up with cubicle walls that were four feet tall with an additional foot of open bookshelf space."
—Anna Hill, Architectural Project Manager

WARM LIGHT

"People do move to San Francisco for its natural beauty, and yet you need to work. When we first moved into the building, it was a bad seventies space that felt like an insurance office. If we didn't get approval for the renovation, we would have come in with saws and slashed down the walls inside. We acknowledge that we work really long hours, and we wanted to have a very warm feeling since San Francisco can get cold and foggy. We were very aware of the cubicle height, so we wouldn't obstruct the windows. When we needed private offices, we still didn't go up to the ceilings. Where there were interior walls, we used polycarbonate ribbed plastic to let light in. In fact, I get upset at people that put binders on top of their cubes now, but I can't be the binder police. When I see people get up from their cubes and gather at a public table for lunch with the sun streaming through the window, I think, 'Yup! We planned that!' We utilized every ounce of natural light that's there. The whole place has a honey, warm glow."
—*Jennifer Golub, Client*

Chan Luu

FROM DRAWINGS TO INSTALLATION

"This project was perfect for me since I was requesting to work on a project that I could follow through into construction. This was about more than doing standard construction administration—I wanted to actually build the project with my own hands. A lot of people come to Marmol Radziner because they want to follow a project through and get their hands dirty in a way that is hard to get somewhere else.

"Since I was going to help build the Chan Luu store, during the design process I could think ahead to construction and make changes to the design details. For example, there were two components to the furniture pieces—the steel frames and the wood cabinets. Initially, the metal and wood elements of the cases were tightly integrated, making it more difficult to divide the tasks of fabricating the metal and wood. We were able to remove much of the overlap between the tasks so that we could work on the boxes in the wood shop while the metal shop produced the frames. Ultimately, we moved the metal frames into the store first and then dropped in the wood pieces later; this made for a much faster fabrication process."

—Aaron Brode, Project Architect

MAKING THE BOXES

"The casework was basically a series of wooden boxes. I knew how to make one box at a time, but I didn't have a good idea of what making fifty boxes was like. When the truck showed up with the lumber, it was a truck **full** of lumber. When I saw that, I finally got a sense of the scale.

"The wood came just as raw lumber. We started by milling the lumber—for two to three weeks pushing it through the planer and joiner to get the boards square. It became an assembly line where we made all of the parts separately. I had a few things to figure out and mess up a bit before I got it right, for example, sandblasting the wood. Ideally, you would mill then sandblast the wood, but once the wood is sandblasted, it no longer is dimensionally square. This meant we had to sandblast the pieces once they were completely assembled. We installed the rollers for the drawers before they were sandblasted, but then all of the rollers were completely ruined with sand in them."
—*Aaron Brode, Project Architect*

"Aaron Brode, Tony Monroy, Hubert Plunkett, and I put in a lot of hours in the shop making these cabinets and panels for Chan Luu. There's just a lot of wood, but it went very fast. Hubert and Tony from our wood shop came in and did the tongue-and-groove solid birch paneling incredibly quickly."
—*Brent Bryan, Wood Shop Manager*

Around the time we were working on Chan Luu's home, her jewelry business started outgrowing her downtown showroom. Chan's jewelry was very colorful, raw, and organic—certainly not minimal in any traditional sense. When commissioned to design her new store we saw it as a space that was both in contrast and in harmony with her designs. Ultimately, this led to a design where all of the elements in the store were simple and cleanly detailed, yet natural and raw.

Each piece of Chan's jewelry is unique, and we wanted to keep that handmade sensibility in her store. Because the design centered on the wood paneling and custom display cases, choosing the right wood with the right finish became very important. In the Kaufmann House restoration,

Detail of relationship between steel bases and natural birch boxes

Detail of blackened steel base

WOOD CASES ON A LARGER SCALE
AT THE HENNESSY + INGALLS BOOKSTORE

The Hennessy + Ingalls bookstore in Santa Monica has always been our primary source for great art and architecture books. When the store moved to a new location in 2003, we were thrilled that the owner asked us to design their new space. While this store was at a very different scale than Chan Luu, both designs revolved around a basic wood box. Hennessey + Ingalls has an immense collection, over 50,000 volumes, that we had to organize in just 8,200 square feet. As the design concept, we inserted an articulated wood box into the existing concrete shell of the space. The wood box in turn holds all of the casework—essentially hundreds of smaller wood boxes.

"The Chan Luu store was like a jewel, but Hennessey and Ingalls was like jewelry in a mass-produced scale. It had a tight budget and was all casework. Every piece of casework is just a box, and the trick is to see how to make the boxes quickly. As the general contractor on the project, we had to find the easiest and cheapest way to do that en masse. I remember showing up one day when they were delivering half of the casework for the entire store at once. Box upon box upon box was delivered. When the installation was complete, I think the owner hired the Santa Monica High School football team to move the books from the old store location around the corner."

—*Daniel Monti, Architectural Project Manager, Hennessy + Ingalls*

we used a natural birch veneer, which is fairly uncommon. Typically, birch is used in its pure white or red variety, taking only from the outer wood and inner core of the tree respectively. Natural birch, however, combines cuts from both the white and red sections of wood in a tree, so the wood appears more earthy and rich. At Chan Luu, we used large pieces of birch so that they had both the red and white tones in significant quantity.

Once we decided to use solid natural birch, our in-house wood shop made many material samples to get the correct rough, tactile finish to the wood. In the end, we selected a wire-brushed finish that we then sandblasted and oiled to create the natural feel that matched Chan's jewelry. Sandblasting caused the wood to hold the oil, which is rare for birch, and maintain the rich, dark brown-orange tone. This color and texture has a strong effect on the experience of the store.

The jewelry cases have simple and clean details, both in how we designed and fabricated them. Where the blackened steel bases and solid wood meet in the cases, we left a gap between the materials. It seemed honest to expose those connections in our building process. Keeping with that raw feeling, we were lucky that the store had wonderful existing concrete floors that provided an ideal backdrop for the cases. We stained the existing floor, so it retained all of the imperfections that time imparts. The rough, earthy quality of the materials contrasts to the more controlled modern aesthetic of the space itself.

Hilltop Studio

SYSTEMS INTEGRATION

When we're working on glass pavilions with open floor plans, as is so often the case with modern buildings, we face the inherent complexity of where to hide technical systems in buildings that have so few solid walls. In recent years, the complexity and sheer number of building systems have increased dramatically. The Hilltop Studio is a perfect example of this—essentially a glass box that now had to take on additional conduit and wiring for mechanized screen operations, televisions, phone systems, stereo equipment, security equipment, and computers.

Squeezing these systems into the walls requires an inordinate amount of planning. On a standard construction project, those decisions are made in the field in a relatively informal way. When there is not enough space to get it all in, we can't take such a loose approach. Without careful planning, the plumber will take up too much space in the wall, or the heating and cooling subcontractor will eat up the entire space that is available, leaving nothing for the other trades.

Slowing down to integrate these different systems is just one element of modern construction that takes longer to build than a traditional-styled home. Despite the deceptive simplicity of clean lines and minimal materials, it takes more care, planning, and, quite frankly, money to achieve. Less is indeed more.

When we first walked the Hilltop site, we were taken aback that we were in this quirky yet modern home that we never knew existed in our city. This site is a prime example of the modernist treasures hidden in Los Angeles. We were almost more shocked to learn that the original architect, Thornton Ladd, designed the home while he was still a student at the University of Southern California. Over five years in the early fifties, he meticulously planned the mountain-top site, including a 6,700-square-foot house for his mother and a 1,300-square-foot detached studio for himself. Spreading out over five acres, the project overlooks Pasadena and the Rose Bowl. Nearly half a century later, the home's new owner asked us to update the small studio and convert the space into a modern guest house.

Ladd's design integrated indoor and outdoor spaces and took advantage of the dramatic views. At the same time, the studio felt like the work of a student with really interesting ideas but perhaps not quite all of the technical capabilities necessary to pull it off. Our goal was to understand what Ladd was trying to do and push his concept to the fullest.

Ladd's original studio was very sympathetic to the new use as a guest house. We did not need to change any of the overall spatial planning of the studio, and instead we focused on clearly defining this glass tree house. We essentially gutted the building down to the steel and concrete structure, leaving just the skeleton. Then we came back in and refined the layers and finishes of the original design to create a glass jewel box in the trees.

Inside the building, we changed the materials, bringing in warm maple casework and cedar flooring. We converted what was once a storage basement into a minimalist guest room inspired by Japanese design. To emphasize the connection to the treetops, our metal shop made

Mechanized sliding privacy shades along the metal catwalk

Detail of sliding shades

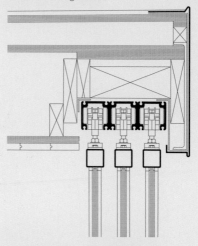

ON-SITE FABRICATION
"There are no off-the-shelf door or window systems in that building at all. The project architect, Chris Lawson, and Scott Enge, from the metal shop, really worked out all of the detailing and fabrication of the sliding doors, which were quite tricky to build. Scott basically invented the hardware for the huge ten-foot pivot door in the basement and engineered it to work; it feels like it weighs five pounds, but it's probably one thousand pounds. Ultimately, Chris became the assistant site super on the project. Having him design a lot of the metal work in the office and then follow it out into the field really made a big difference."
—Scott Walter, Architectural Project Manager

pivoting doors in this tatami room that open onto a new cantilevered cedar deck. We added a window at the end of the galley kitchen that completely opens the space, reinforcing the ideas of the floating, overlapping planes suspended in the trees.

Large sliding glass doors and privacy shades surrounded the structure to create geometric patterns and to allow for a cross breeze. Many of the sliders were no longer operable. Our in-house metal fabricators set up shop on site to create the entire steel window system from scratch, with each window custom fit to its space in the building. We replaced the damaged fabric screens with new translucent shades made from rice paper sandwiched between two sheets of glass. Whereas the original fabric screens were opaque, we introduced more transparency with the new shades to reinforce the connection to the trees. We also mechanized the screens to eliminate the need to venture out onto a catwalk to slide the shades manually. Now with the flick of a switch, the shades slide along their tracks, changing the subtle, dappled light of the studio.

Hilltop is a favorite project in our office, in large part because the studio is a small, quiet gem with a powerful interaction of indoor and outdoor living. But also, hidden in the studio's understated elegance, behind the simplicity of the lines and materials, lie refined assemblies and complicated fabrications.

Before

FLEXIBILITY IN RESTORATION

In reality, not every mid-century building is historic and demands the same meticulous restoration as a project like the Kaufmann House. For many mid-century homes, rehabilitation standards provide the flexibility to make these older buildings work as houses that support current needs. If we do not embrace the need for such changes, these buildings will be condemned to insensitive alterations or destruction as owners try to meet their current needs. A house will become useless without the day-to-day living pragmatics such as heating and cooling systems that actually work, a convenient kitchen, or the technological integration of Internet connections, stereos, and flat screen televisions.

When we approach a project with an older, potentially historic, building, we look at the project and evaluate the relative historic importance (is this a truly historic resource or just a beautiful older building?); the current physical condition (how have the structural and finish materials held up over time?); the proposed use (what are the goals and needs of our clients?); and mandatory code requirements (does the building contain toxic materials or unsound structural systems?). Juggling these issues, we determine the appropriate changes and degree of latitude we need to alter the existing conditions.

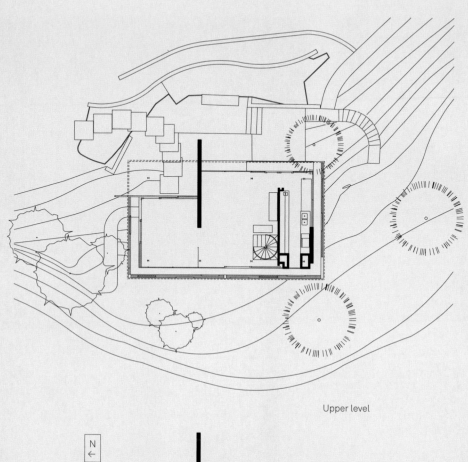

Upper level

N
←

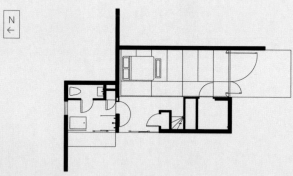

Lower level

82

ON-SITE FABRICATION

"Because we worked with existing conditions at Hilltop, not new construction, we fabricated the windows and doors on-site. The building is fifty years old, so nothing is plumb or square. A perfect example is the two big doors in the tatami room. One of those doors is five-eighths of an inch wider at the top than the bottom because those sheer walls were out of whack. In order to have no reveals and scribe spaces, everything had to be built out of square. I gave Chris Lawson some general parameters, and he designed the details for the windows and doors. He did a good job. My personal aesthetic is that I try to be as dainty as possible, maybe that's because weighing in at over two hundred pounds, I'm the opposite. But Chris worked with bigger sections that were really…manly."

—*Scott Enge, Metal Shop Manager*

Before

THE TATAMI ROOM
"We did quite a bit of research into Japanese architecture. We designed the new cedar deck to continue the proportions of the tatami mat as it proceeds outside, so the deck feels like an extension of the mat. The black cloth bands of the tatami mat become the exposed steel frames of the deck, and we dropped in cedar planks flush to the top of the steel to create a flat, mat-like surface."
—*Scott Walter, Architectural Project Manager*

Glencoe Residence

THE ARCHITECT'S HOME
"Because this was a great opportunity for Ron to explore his vision, I was hands off during the design process. I didn't want to interfere with the purity of his ideas. I would show up and be blown away. 'Wow! I get to live here?' He created a beautiful home."
—*Robin Cottle*

"Ron was able to explore his beliefs in a very pure way. It gave him the platform to free himself from some of the burden that you have with a client and get at some of those core ideas. It's very pure, very direct, very simple, very understated, very subtle. There is a tendency among architects to overcompensate when they do things for themselves. In Ron's house, you see a level of maturity and confidence in its understatement and raw geometric simplicity."
—*Leo*

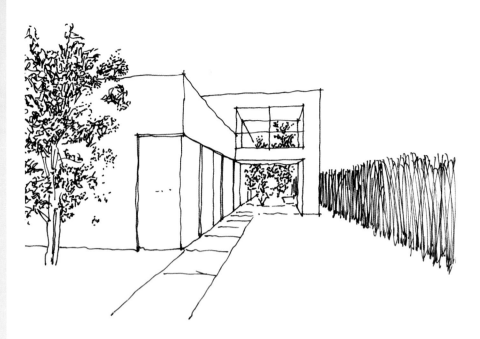

"I like modern architecture that is a bit more of the earth. I like humanmade forms, orthogonal forms, that are in natural colors. I like when architecture is not so definitely set off from the landscape, which is why most of our buildings are brown and green, almost to a point where it has become an inside joke. When we first started practicing, I remember proposing green-colored buildings, and it was extremely hard to convince clients to go with it. Things have changed. Now it's more acceptable, and we have more examples to show clients how well it can work. I was once in a book club with a man named Brown Greene, and I thought he was such a lucky person to have that name."
—*Ron*

We are fortunate to work on many wonderful projects, so when Ron decided to make a home for his family, he did not need to cram in every design idea he ever had. Instead, he explored his core principles of integrating with the natural surroundings. Ron started the process by himself, sketching out ideas almost exclusively in plan and section. In some projects, we move to building models very quickly. For budgetary purposes, Ron designed the project on paper, creating only one rendering to show his wife, Robin Collie. At 45 feet by 130 feet, the narrow nature of the lot greatly dictated the possibilities for the 2,700 square-foot home. Conceptually, Ron wanted to maximize the interaction between the garden and the house and create both indoor and outdoor rooms. To do that, the house took on a linear quality, designed to be only as wide as the standard two-car garage required by code.

Breaking out of the main linear environment, a strong perpendicular gesture creates the outdoor dining room with a fireplace on the ground floor and the master bedroom on the second floor. That space is open below and mostly transparent above with all of the windows in the bedroom. The recessed L-shape of the second story minimizes the visual impact of the additional floor from the street while defining distinct outdoor spaces. These different layers, combined with the Japanese Black Pine tree we planted behind the outdoor dining area, create a series of screens and veils that help to divide the outdoor spaces while still appearing transparent.

"I remember driving around looking for 'the tree' that had the right sculptural quality. I saw a lot of trees in the hunt for the one with the right scale. I would find one that was a contender and show it to Ron, and he'd say it wasn't right. Then he said he had seen a tree that was a possibility. When we went back to see that tree, we immediately knew it was the right one. When it came time to install the Japanese pine, it was amazing. We craned it over the house and set it in place."
—*Daniel Monti, Architectural Project Manager*

Second Floor

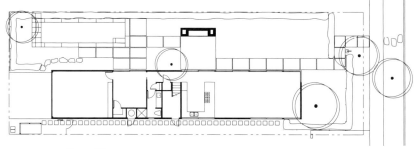

Ground Floor

To emphasize the integration of the outdoor spaces, the home has no traditional front door; instead, an entrance in a landscaped hedge wall along the sidewalk acts as the front door for both the house and garden. Once visitors enter the garden, they are in the home. By utilizing full-height glass that runs down the length of the house, the design allows the landscape, rather than the physical building, to define the edge of the living space.

The natural tones of the home's straightforward material palette reinforce a connection to the surrounding landscape. Our cabinet shop fabricated walnut kitchen cabinets that bring a rich brown tone into the great room to compliment the exposed concrete floors. Upstairs, the walnut continues as hardwood flooring and built-in casework. All of the elements come together in cleanly detailed material transitions that look deceptively simple. As the builders of the home, we were able to work through the significant construction challenge of hiding connections and making dissimilar materials flush with one another.

This home, in many ways, echoes the Kaufmann House restoration in our ability to work on the total environment of the site. We designed not only the home itself but the landscape and furniture as well. Then our staff built the home, fabricated the furniture, and executed the entire project down to the last detail. Perhaps because of that breadth of work, this home also became very important for the office, bringing in new and interesting projects.

DESTRUCTION
"Demolition of the old house on the site was on September 11, 2001. I remember waking up, listening to the news, and seeing the events unfold. Eventually, I went to the job site and the demo guy was already there. He was a huge burly guy, and we shared a few words. Then we had this eerie silence between the two of us watching them tear this house apart."
—Daniel Monti, Architectural Project Manager

THE OUTDOOR FIREPLACE

"In the original drawings, I had a fireplace at the end of the indoor living room. The fireplace never really worked—I just couldn't get the massing right. At an office lunch, I presented the design, and there was some good feedback. I'm not sure if someone exactly said it or if just talking about it helped me get past it, but that was when I decided that maybe I didn't need the indoor fireplace. That change made all the difference. Leaving only the outdoor fireplace remaining in the design really refocused the house to the outside. In the living room, you can still participate in the fireplace visually, but it draws you outside to interact physically with the fire."
—*Ron*

Counter sub-frame

DETAILS

"Ron really wanted the stainless steel kitchen countertop with integral sink to be detailed so that there were no joints across the entire piece. Making that work was the hardest aspect of the cabinetry in the entire house. If we had just taken measurements, it never would have worked while still maintaining the seamless design. The entire countertop came in one piece, including the backsplash, so it was approximately fifteen feet by thirteen feet. We had to build the plywood subframe on site, haul it out in one piece, drive it to the shop on the back of a pickup, fit the stainless countertop in place, weld the sink, bring the frame back to the site, and then drop the counter into place. That was the only way for it to work as a seamless design. Everything came out just fine, but I did have a couple of sleepless nights."
—*Brent Bryan, Cabinet Shop Manager*

"I learned a lot about detailing—how things go together and how to put a house together that's well built. Trying to do a project that's good quality is a real challenge because not everyone is on the same page about getting the best subs, the best craftsmen. It's a constant battle to do that. The appreciation to push to get what you want in construction is one of the biggest things I took from the firm when I started my own practice."
—*Daniel Monti, Architectural Project Manager*

PLAYFUL MODERNISM

"Glencoe was a great family house. I loved that we were able to combine the play area with the living area and keep an eye on the kids while cooking. That was so successful for us, as a family, that we were inspired to expand this idea for our Vienna Way home."
—*Robin Cottle*

Marmol Radziner Furniture

Previous spread: Club chair (left),
Walnut dining chair (right)

Left: Kings Road Group sling chair
Below: Kings Road Group child's chair

IN-HOUSE PRODUCTION

"I love that we do furniture. The scale, the craft—it's interesting, understandable. You can think of it in one whole thought, as opposed to a whole house. The furniture is very manageable, and it's made from solid wood, which is rewarding. The craftsmen in our shop desire to make objects, and the furniture are self-contained pieces requiring more than just making boxes for cabinets."
—*Brent Bryan, Wood Shop Manager*

Kings Road Group sofa under production

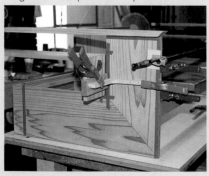

Our early forays into furniture were at the request of clients, who often asked us to design and build a particular piece of furniture in our cabinet and metal shops. Many of our projects also had built-in pieces, like sofas and banquettes. Occasionally, for our restoration projects, we would reproduce a piece that was no longer in production. In that spirit, the Friends of the Schindler House approached us in 2001 to fabricate and market authorized reproductions of R.M. Schindler's Kings Road Group, which we happily embraced.

We all loved the simple materials and relaxed yet elegant nature of Schindler's designs, but when Ron started looking at pieces of furniture to use at his own home on Glencoe, he didn't find available retail pieces that seemed like the right fit. Given furniture's importance in shaping the experience and scale of a house, Ron felt like it was a natural progression to design furniture for his new house.

While the pieces for Glencoe eventually became our retail furniture line, Ron initially started working based on the basic proportions and materiality of that particular house. He would find it very difficult to design a generic piece of furniture without visualizing it in a specific space. We only considered selling the pieces in a retail context after Glencoe

Kings Road Group line

Low lounge

Low lounge prototype

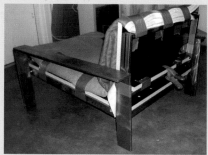

THE LIMBO OF THE LOW LOUNGE
"The low lounge was always intended to be by the pool. You're low to the ground when you're at the pool. Proportionally, it looks right to me. Some people feel it is too low and want us to make it taller. It looks terrible taller. They should just buy a different chair. But really, the low lounge was designed for me, exactly the way I wanted it for my own house. It never even occurred to me that the chair was low."
—*Ron*

"The low lounge is a very complicated piece that required a lot of refinement, particularly in the leg detail and its relationship to the planes of the chair. It's an homage to Rietvelt's crate lounge that uses different planes, but it has a thin profile in steel that creates a very different feel. It was kind of like the limbo— how low can we go with it. Some people really don't like it, and some people like it a lot. It's really about the region where it was made, with a certain casualness of California living that generally involves a pool."
—*Michael Ned Holte, Furniture Designer*

received so much press and subsequent inquiries about the furniture.

To support the integration of the indoors and outdoors at Glencoe, Ron developed furniture for the entire project, including both interior and exterior spaces. While the exterior pieces are primarily from stainless steel and teak and the indoor pieces primarily from walnut and fabric, they all share similar designs. We started working on the outdoor dining table first, and that piece defined the profile, details, and proportions of the entire suite of furniture. On that and several other pieces, our metal and cabinet shops made several mock-ups and prototypes to refine the style, details, and production process for the furniture. We pushed the tolerance of the materials to form thin, low profiles in the pieces, creating a refined aesthetic.

Ron made all of the pieces from solid materials. We chose solid stainless steel for its strength and beauty and used a natural-stained walnut that would stand out against the dark stain of Glencoe's built-in walnut cabinetry. The pieces are incredibly heavy, probably too heavy, but we like the directness of using the solid materials that demonstrate how they are crafted. The furniture is like our buildings — cleanly detailed and built.

Since launching the Glencoe furniture as a retail line, we made subtle alterations to the original designs to make them easier to reproduce. We are proud that what started as designs for Ron and his family now fills homes and gardens around the country.

Hubert Plunkett fabricates a walnut dining table

PROTOTYPING

Our design-build process greatly facilitated the prototyping and development of the furniture line. We would often meet with Scott Enge and Brent Bryan, the managers of our metal and cabinet shops, to work through rough mock-ups or discuss how the fabrication process would affect the design of the furniture pieces.

"Cold rolled stainless steel flatbars are solid sections of metal that come in fixed rectangular square dimensions. Only certain proportions are available, so if you're going to build a piece of furniture, it's got to be from one of those dimensions. We designed the first outdoor dining chair with beautiful proportions. I think it had half-inch by one-inch and half-inch by two inch sections, so it was almost platonically harmonic—squares, double squares, geometric relationships. We mocked up just the frame of the chair, and it weighed over eighty pounds and took two people to move. We went through three or four reductions of size and materials until we got to the final outdoor dining chair. The profile couldn't get much thinner and still stand up. Between Ron and the furniture project manager Michale Holte, they got pretty good at pushing the envelope of function and form. I think the furniture really represents the development of an idea as much as anything that this office has ever done. It started with a concept, and between Brent and myself doing prototypes, sometimes six or seven iterations, we got to the final design."
—Scott Enge, Metal Shop Manager

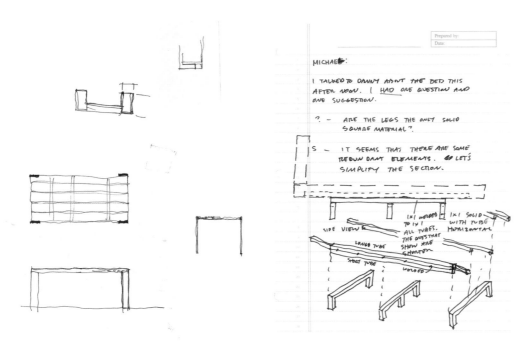

Prepared by: _____
Date: _____

MICHAEL:

I TALKED TO DANNY ABOUT THE BED THIS AFTER NOON. I HAD ONE QUESTION AND ONE SUGGESTION.

?. - ARE THE LEGS THE ONLY SOLID SQUARE MATERIAL?

S - IT SEEMS THAT THERE ARE SOME REDUNDANT ELEMENTS. LET'S SIMPLIFY THE SECTION.

SIDE VIEW

1x1 WELDED TO 1x1 ALL TUBES. THE ONES THAT SHOW ARE SHORTER

1x1 SOLID WITH TUBE HORIZONTAL

LONG TUBE

SHORT TUBE   WELDED

Desert House low table

ALTERATIONS FOR THE RETAIL MARKET
"My part was working out the production bugs and trying to control the costs with endless meetings with Brent and Scott to make details that would lend themselves to production. Most of our pieces are very detailed, and we racked our brains to get the same effect without using things like hand-constructed brackets that had precisely-fitted set screws. Our original walnut dining chair had brackets that had to nest and align perfectly so the set screw could tie the upholstery to the frame, leaving a quarter inch gap between the frame and the back. The effect is really beautiful, but it made the chairs a little wobbly and took three hours to put together. On that chair, we eliminated the metal elements and used mortise-and-tenon joinery in a way that still looked refined but was also more stable and easier to produce."
—Daniella Wilson, Furniture Designer

IN-HOUSE PRODUCTION
"I'm still learning about how I want to make the furniture pieces, and I'm definitely getting a lot faster. It can become monotonous to make the same thing over and over again, but just the fact that it becomes easier is gratifying. You feel like you actually are becoming more of a master. And the luxury of working in five-eighths of an inch thick solid stainless steel is an extravagance that I don't think you could come by very often other than here. The pieces are pretty squirrelly because stainless bends a lot with heat. You can bend it back, but you just have to know where to apply the heat. Trying to make a line true to the design is a challenge. I like making the retail pieces, but the custom furniture work is my favorite because it's original — I eat it up."
—James McDemas, Metal Fabricator

Ward Luu Residence

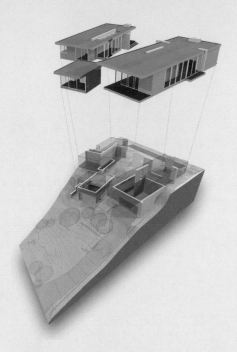

SITE CHALLENGES

"The lot was the biggest challenge — in a canyon, on a small street, in a quiet neighborhood, and on an extremely steep site. Getting materials unloaded was very difficult. You can imagine unloading on the driveway and hand-carrying materials around the site. The driveway was so steep that at one point the hydraulics on a forklift went out. The forklift went careening across the street, jumped three feet in the air, and the concrete block shattered as it came crashing down. Luckily no one was hurt. The house was also carefully sited to preserve the trees. We had to put up barriers and remind workers to stay away from the trees. At times, the cantilevers went out and were practically touching the trees. It was difficult to work around them, but it was well worth it."

—Ross Yerian, *Construction Project Manager*

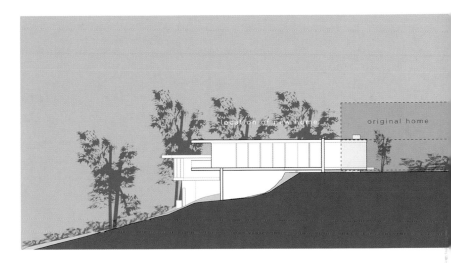

original home

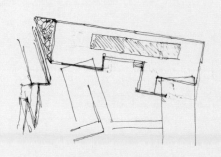

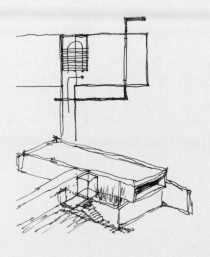

When we first saw the site of the Ward Luu Residence, we found an existing house sitting on the upper plateau of a steep lot. The old, dark two-story building seemed to be nervously peering into the adjacent backyards. This uneasy relationship to the neighbors felt at odds with the serene Rustic Canyon neighborhood, filled with beautiful homes by noted architects such as Ray Kappe, Pierre Koenig, and A. Quincy Jones. For the new home, we knew we needed a far more harmonious solution — one that engaged the vertical lot and natural surroundings.

We started by making study models looking at different configurations on the site. We quickly felt that the most natural resolution was to push the house down into the earth. We developed a conceptual design that integrated with the hillside, exploiting the lot's steep slope and shifting the home forward and away from the neighboring yards. We decided to settle the new house into the site and created a series of heavy boxes nestled into the hillside with lighter metal and glass pavilions floating above.

We arranged the home's 4,000 square feet into distinct volumes according to the client's requirements of public, private, and work areas. These three separate volumes perch delicately atop solid masses of burnished concrete block embedded within the hillside. Starting above a natural wetland occurring at the bottom of the hillside, the main entry stair rises between two heavy concrete forms. At the top of the stairs, the

SELECTING THE MASONRY

At the early stages of design, the embedded masses didn't need to be concrete block—they just needed to be conceptually heavy because they were coming out of the earth. The base walls could have been stone or block or even poured concrete. We studied a variety of block types, ranging from craggy split-faced textures to smooth and sand-blasted finishes. We also looked at block in an array of colors, from pale white to warm gray. Finally, we decided to use white concrete blocks with burnished faces for its unique beauty and ability to play off the rustic nature of the site. Burnishing the block removes the outer layer of a standard concrete block to create a smooth surface. As Stephanie Hobbs, the architectural project manager, explains, "It's like taking a cheese slicer to the concrete block."

In the end, the burnished concrete blocks play a key role in the structure and design of the Ward Luu Residence. Both physically and metaphorically, the blocks anchor the house by providing mass as the buildings emerge from the earth, and counterbalancing the light cantilevered pavilions resting above. By continuing exterior walls and structural elements inside the home, we used the burnished concrete block to strengthen the connection between indoors and outdoors.

glazed entry hall bridges the public and private volumes of the house while revealing the flow of the landscape to the backyard. In contrast to the heavy massing of the bases, the light-filled glazed pavilions seem to float within the treetops.

From a construction perspective, this pairing of embedded block boxes with floating glass pavilions became one of the most difficult projects our staff had built to date. The project started as two separate buildings in the masonry phase that later were connected by a structural steel bridge. Our site staff had to field measure everything to make sure it all fit. Even a quarter of an inch disparity would be problematic. At the same time, the roof structure was very complicated because the recessed shade pockets made for a complex structural system.

Now, several years removed from the excavations and masonry, we like going back to this house and following the progression of the site and form as it rises from a rustic natural landscape to the defined, human-made elements in the treetops.

MANAGING THE MASONRY

At one dollar to burnish each side of a block, we wanted to burnish only the exposed faces of the concrete. To place an accurate material order, we needed to figure out exactly how many of each type of block was needed for the structure. The project architects Brad Lang and Patrick McHugh drew diagrams for every masonry wall and then color-coded the diagrams to show whether each block was burnished on one side, two sides, or three sides, and whether each was eight or twelve inches wide. Once the burnished block arrived on-site, mason Clive Christie began work installing the stacked concrete walls.

"Ward Luu was such a complex, tough job. We had quite a lot of trouble with the block—there was a lot more variation in the material than I expected. The burnishing took one sixteenth of an inch off of a face, so if you laid a block that was burnished on two sides on top of a block that was burnished on one side, of course the sides weren't quite matching. Also, we found some height differences, which meant the problem was in the forms. Luckily, since we were using a flush joint, that didn't really show up. The joint helped conceal any inconsistencies. If the joint had been recessed, it might have been a problem."
—*Clive Christie, Mason*

"A lot of the success in this project was building it ourselves, with our own labor. When we needed more control over the work, we could slow down to get it right. We were very fortunate to have Clive Christie as a master mason on the site. Clive would figure out how to do something, and then he would teach it to the labor staff. Once people understood and bought into the vision of the project, it really started to click. It turned out that one laborer, Joaquin Mendoza, was very detail-oriented, so he became 'the guy' to do many of the specific parts of the job."
—*Ross Yerian, Construction Project Manager*

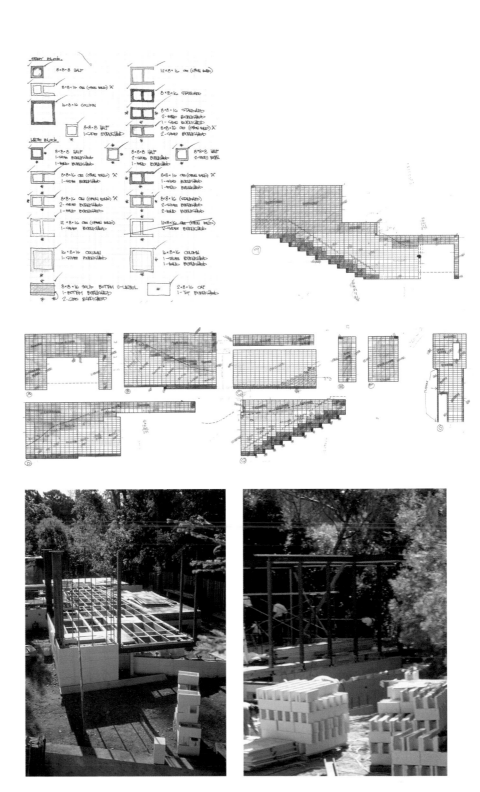

FINISH MATERIALS AS STRUCTURE

Masonry walls are both the structural support for the building and an exposed, finished surface requiring careful detailing. Concrete block is typically installed with a running bond pattern, where each row of blocks is offset from the previous row. With running bond, each block does not have to be perfectly aligned. But when you stack the block, as we did in the Ward Luu Residence, the vertical lines became very important to control. Because we had so much stacked block, and in front of such large excavations, the simple act of aligning a vertical joint, of controlling that line, became very complicated. The level of finish detail and the quality of the installation are little things that one might not notice, but they are some of the things that make us most proud.

"At Ward Luu, the walls are both the finished product and what holds up the building. Wood structures are much more forgiving, but concrete block and steel—once they go in, they don't like to be moved. We were able to build this home like a cabinet. It has that level of finish, but at the scale of an entire building."
—*Ross Yerian, Construction Project Manager*

AFTER CONSTRUCTION

"My Tuesday morning meetings on the site in the freezing cold in Rustic Canyon are the first things that come to mind when I think of this project. Every week, for a year and a half, at seven in the morning. You get so connected to the people and to the site. The hardest part of the project was the day when I couldn't go back to the house anymore. After working on it for two and a half years, that was the day when the house became theirs, not ours. It's painful. I can't just go there whenever I want."
—*Stephanie Hobbs, Architectural Project Manager*

"We took a lot of risks with the house, and any time you do that, it is going to be idiosyncratic. It's never perfect, and that comes with doing a first home of its type. So you live in it and realize things and change things. It's an ongoing design challenge, not a static living experience. For example, we built the house with very dark floors to contrast with the light walls and burnished block. I learned that having dark floors and a shedding Airedale dog are mutually exclusive. We recently stripped down the floors to their natural white oak finish, and that already feels like a much more honest solution."
—*John Ward, Client*

TreePeople Center
for Community Forestry

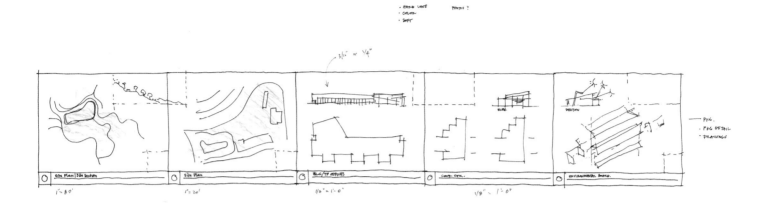

Our involvement with TreePeople goes back nearly two decades. Long ago, we interviewed with TreePeople in their search for a partner to design a new home base. Inspired by TreePeople's mission to rebuild the urban forest, we convinced them that our passion about environmental responsiveness compensated for our youth and lack of experience. In 1990, when we began designing TreePeople, the concepts of sustainability were far from the mainstream. It took visionary interest and commitment from TreePeople and its founder, Andy Lipkis, to champion the sustainability of the Center. From the very beginning, we added the environment to our standard design concerns of aesthetics, functionality, and economics. We kept those four criteria in mind throughout the project as we designed the master plan, buildings, technical systems, and materials.

Our initial work with TreePeople was to develop the master plan for their site located within the forty-five acres of Coldwater Canyon Park in the Santa Monica Mountains. We found in TreePeople a great kinship in recognizing the necessity of confronting environmental issues. TreePeople created a dynamic and collaborative approach to developing the site. Over the course of the project, we worked with a team of environmental thinkers, including a group that did the architectural programming, the UCLA professor Richard Schoen on sustainable design technologies, an outside landscape designer, and Arup as the structural and mechanical, electrical, and plumbing engineers. As we learned more about sustainability, the theories behind solar orientation, natural air flows, and water

SITE APPROVALS

"In many ways, entitlements and permits became the most difficult part of the process. At one point, I counted that between all of the different agencies, we had over one hundred individual clearances for different permits. We were working with nearly every agency you could imagine, from the Department of Transportation to the City's Street Trees Division. There were a lot of code issues as well because we were trying to build what would amount to a 19,000 square-foot campus in a public park along the Mulholland Scenic Parkway. It was really a testament to TreePeople's reputation in the community that we were able to get the project permitted. The surrounding community is known for critically reviewing even the smallest house, but they were excited to approve this project."
—*Bobby Rees, Architectural Project Manager*

management became primary considerations when we designed the master plan. We had to be careful siting the buildings because not only did we have to deal with issues of sustainability but we also learned that the site was essentially all former landfill and therefore had challenging soil issues. When locating the Environmental Learning Center, we left some space between the building and the hillside to allow light to enter the back of the structures. Since that building would be the most consistently used structure on the site, we oriented it to face south to maximize the natural lighting. The overall site is designed to funnel the rainwater into an underground cistern for use in watering the landscape.

After we determined the master plan and building locations, we began designing the Environmental Learning Center and the Conference Center buildings. Conceptually, we wanted the architecture to embrace the surrounding landscape and blur the boundaries between interior and exterior space. Transparent walls, floating roofs, and wood beams break the building envelope to create connections to the mature tree canopy. While we knew glass was notoriously inefficient, we felt using large windows and glass doors was important to create these connections and bring natural air and light into the buildings. To compensate for the inefficiency of glass, we hooded the windows with sunshades and roof overhangs and used high-efficiency glazing to allow light through without significant solar heat gain.

Construction of the underground cistern

WATER MANAGEMENT

With TreePeople's emphasis on promoting sustainable water management, it is fitting that the site sits just off Mulholland Drive, the iconic Los Angeles route named after William Mullholland, the grandfather of Los Angeles's water system and the Los Angeles Aqueduct. In our city's current water management system, the Department of Public Works spends millions of dollars on storm drainage that channels all runoff into concrete storm drains that swiftly whisk the water away to the ocean. At the same time, the Department of Water and Power spends millions of dollars importing fresh water via Mulholland's aqueduct to support the City's usage.

Responding to TreePeople's mission and this dependence on water from Mulholland's aqueduct, we knew that storm-water management should play a central role in our design. We designed the buildings to have floating, butterfly-shaped roofs that capture and transport rainwater to an underground storage cistern in the center of the site. The cistern holds up to 250,000 gallons of rainwater to use for irrigation or other needs on site. It also acts as a demonstration model for TreePeople's advocacy for a citywide system of cisterns and infiltrators to help capture storm water runoff and recharge the natural, underground aquifer.

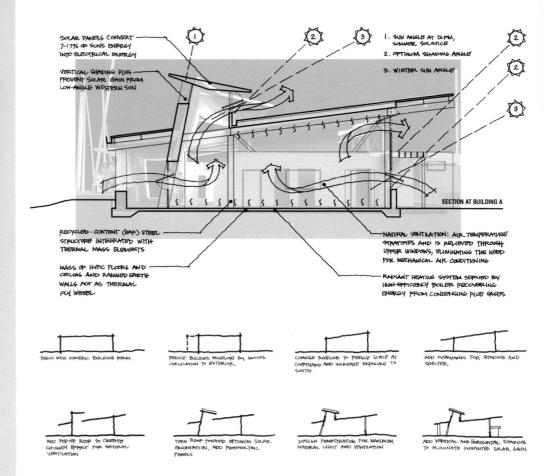

WATER MANAGEMENT

"The Department of Building and Safety is behind the times and works to support the Department of Public Works and get all of the runoff water into the gutters. They are most concerned about water runoff in hillside areas because landslides and unstable soil are more likely to cause problems there. We showed that we could do a better job by managing the water on site rather than funneling the water to the street gutters. By code, we were required to have the roof water and parking lot runoff feed into the storm drains. However at TreePeople, we not only designed the buildings and site to funnel that water into the cistern but we also designed a swale, a shallow drainage channel, to pick up the water running off the slope to channel it into the cistern. TreePeople's good will with the local government is the main reason we got elements like the cistern through city approvals. For the cistern, we received a modification to the building code, whereas typically this would require a variance, if it would be allowed at all. While a variance would have involved a public hearing and taken at least six months, a modification was $100 and staff-approved."
—*Bobby Rees, Architectural Project Manager*

We also used the passive solar design principal of thermal massing to moderate the temperature of the buildings. In the cool months, thick, fifty-percent fly ash concrete slabs and walls absorb heat by day and radiate heat at night. During the hot months, the inverse occurs—the mass cools at night and absorbs heat from the air during the day. The project team inventoried the materials from the existing buildings to incorporate them into the design. The concrete formwork for the massive walls were made, in part, from wood found on the site. Similarly, we used the one hundred-year-old lumber from the original fire station on site as exterior solar shades for the Conference Center.

TreePeople represented the opportunity to immerse ourselves in the concepts of green-building technologies. The Conference Center was one of the early projects registered with LEED, which recently received LEED Gold Certification. We hope that the Center continues to facilitate TreePeople's mission to inspire Angelenos to take personal responsibility for our collective urban environment.

The Accelerated School of
South Los Angeles (TAS)

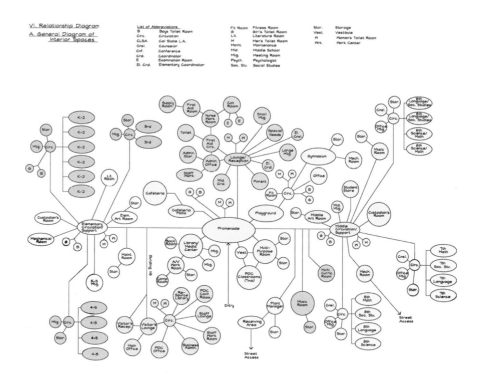

PROGRAMMING AND THE COMMUNITY

Once we got the commission, we started developing the architectural program for the school with extensive outreach to the community and staff. We ran community meetings in both English and Spanish in what became a very personal process. When we were sitting down and speaking with a small group in the evening, we could begin to understand people's needs. We could tell from the energy of the parents that showed up that it was going to be a wonderful school.

"The programming phase was filled with bubbles and diamonds and squares and question marks, all addressing different concerns and different needs. The firm must have spent a couple hundred hours doing the programming, meeting with the community, students, parents, and faculty. We convened a meeting of the school as a whole, including all of the parents and staff, to approve the general concepts. We were committed to having an inclusive, transparent process."
—*Jonathan Williams, Co-founder, The Accelerated School*

YOUTH/NAIVETE

"There were a lot of overwhelming aspects to the project, and we did not have a lot of experience with running a building program. In terms of scale, the project was also new to Marmol Radziner. It was so complex, but because we were learning together, there was a lot of camaraderie."
—*Kevin Sved, Co-founder, The Accelerated School*

Our memories of the Los Angeles riots had not yet faded when we first heard of the young charter school. TAS was looking to build a new campus in the heart of the neighborhood that went up in flames a few years earlier. The founders of TAS, Kevin Sved and Jonathan Williams, had an impassioned vision for a school that provides powerful learning experiences for every student and acts as a center for the community that, as the riots exposed, greatly lacked in resources. TAS and its board hosted a competition to select the architects for their new campus.

In the design competition, we surveyed the neighborhood and photographed everything that we loved, that showed aspirations for community in this distressed neighborhood. Once we received the commission, we began the architectural programming and master planning for the school by engaging the school's teachers, students, families, and neighbors to ensure we understood the needs and desires of the community. In Los Angeles, most public schools follow a traditional suburban model of one-story buildings spread across large sites. According to this model, to meet TAS's programmatic needs, the school would have required nearly thirty acres of land. Yet, TAS had only 4.4

BUILDING IN SOUTH LOS ANGELES
"Including the community from the very beginning helped with getting support from the neighbors. Even during the construction process, which closed off streets and put dust and dirt into the air, we had very few complaints. People enjoy having this building in their community—it makes them feel like we've got a little piece of Hollywood here in South Los Angeles."
—Jonathan Williams, Co-founder, The Accelerated School

acres in the heart of South Los Angeles. We approached the conceptual design with an "every space counts" philosophy, whereby every horizontal surface took on programmatic roles as an opportunity for formal and impromptu gathering and learning.

We went through three major schematic revisions and ultimately chose a design that struck a balance of providing open space without stacking all of the building mass into imposing structures. In the final design, the medium-rise structures on the site's two commercial edges cascade down to a residential scale in the large, partially enclosed courtyard space. At the same time, the ramplike quality of the roofs creates additional spaces for education and play while allowing for circulation and egress.

This scheme also met two of the primary requirements we regularly heard in community meetings: the need for security and the desire for spaces to serve the neighborhood. As the conceptual anchors of the school, the community spaces, such as the library, gymnasium, auditorium, and health center are on the ground level, close to school entrances for neighborhood access. We had to balance the integration of security requirements with supporting the school's civic mission of fostering

"The design needed to spring organically from the needs of the community and the project constraints from a funding, entitlement, and code perspective. A year into the design, the state passed some of the first large public school construction bonds in over twenty years. When we approached the Los Angeles Unified School District (LAUSD) to request funding for their take of the state bond money, our existing private funding essentially enabled them to double their investment in the school. They couldn't say 'no'.

"Accepting this state bond money meant the entire campus was required to meet Division of the State Architect (DSA) requirements, so suddenly we were designing to a completely different standard. Building vertical, multistory schools is not a big deal in Chicago or New York. But when we were working at TAS, there was no one at DSA here in California who had worked on a multistory new school construction project. Also, we were developing a K–12 educational program, which is not an existing public school model, though it is a very well established private school model. We needed to integrate standard public school design requirements in a K–12 setting, like providing different emergency exits for different age groups.
—*Eric Johnson, Chair, TAS Site Development Committee*

"For public schools to receive certain funding, your design must be approved by the Division of the State Architect (DSA). During the schematic design and design development architectural phases, we had regular meetings with DSA so that nothing would surprise them in our final document sets. These meetings are not standard—they were Leo's idea—and it worked really well. When we submitted to DSA, we filled my entire station wagon with the documents. In the end, DSA approved the design in three months, as they had promised us originally."
—*Jim Burkholder, Architectural Project Manager*

community involvement. We developed a layered facade that provides visual separation from the street, and we focused on creating interaction with the environment in the large internal courtyard. To control campus access, we punctured the facade only at specific entry points.

The scope of work we faced at TAS—from integrating such a broad range of stakeholders to responding to security concerns to the design of special concentric braced frame steel structures—was essentially uncharted territory for us. Typically we work at a residential scale, where we can be involved in every detail. Yet, when the structures get large, as they did at TAS, it becomes more and more taxing to maintain that level of involvement. We worked hard to make sure that we never let the sheer scale of TAS become alienating—we wanted the students and community to be able to look closely at the building, feel the connections of how the building came together, and still be satisfied.

DEDICATION

"I came onto the project after all of the programming work was done, so the client interactions that I had were more about permits and approvals. At the time, I thought it was a great project and great program, but it was really just a project without any other meaning for me until one day right before construction started. We were at the site, and Kevin and Jonathan invited us to the teacher appreciation lunch that the parents were hosting. I practically cried at this luncheon because the parents told stories about how their kids were doing at school and what the teachers did for them. I remember this one woman, who was a domestic worker for a family in Beverly Hills. She told how her daughter was reading the same books that her employer's kids were reading at their fancy prep school. I realized just how great it was to be part of this project. To see what the school meant to these families was touching."
—*Annette Wu, Project Architect*

"One thing that worked really well was the team. Jim and Annette were incredible at doing whatever it took. Ron was very involved in the design in the beginning, then he stepped back once the design was detailed out. Then Leo became the person on point. The quality, the professionalism, and the team-work—no way would it have been built in the short time it was in any other way. That commitment to a project isn't coming because there's a pay check at the end. There was a real commitment to the mission of the organization and to giving the kids the best campus possible."
—*Kevin Sved, Co-Founder, The Accelerated School*

Altamira Ranch

We were a year into designing The Accelerated School when we held a client meeting at our office. A member of TAS's board knew us only in the context of this institutional project and was surprised to see that we had images and models of residences spread out on our walls and tables. "I just bought a bluff-top property in Palos Verdes," he said. "Any idea of what I could do with it?" We went to the nineteen-acre property and saw an expansive site perched above the Pacific Ocean with views in all directions. Before long, we got to work designing a new family home intended for generations to come.

The site itself and the client's background in geology became a major design inspiration. We went through many iterations of the design, but in the end we came back to the concept of the home creating a fissure in the ground and growing out of the earth. This idea comes in large part from the site's location just next to a landslide zone, where the earth twists and turns from frequent geological movement. Beyond the conceptual appeal of hugging low to the ground, the city required a sixteen-foot height limit to protect the neighbor's ocean views. We focused on sculpting the home on the ocean site while keeping the profile low on the street side of the property.

ARCHITECTURAL CONCRETE

"To set up a concrete pour was a four week process. After the pour, the concrete had to cure for another week, and then we could strip away the molds, protect the concrete, and move on. We did many small mock-ups of the mold and then one medium-sized mold. Once we decided on a form strategy, we made a full-size mock-up that was ten feet wide and eleven feet high and included windows and other things that we knew would come up along the way. The mock-ups were very helpful, but at a certain point you just have to go with it and learn with each pour. We did the first pour in the basement and learned from there as we went up in levels. You're really on pins and needles the day of the pour. You never knew what you were going to get."
—*Ross Yerian, Construction Project Manager*

Concrete pour

Front entry hardscape construction

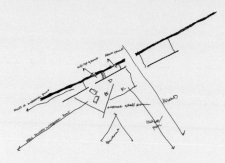

ON-SITE ARCHITECTURE

"I was on site every day, so there were no walls between me and the craftspeople. This level of on-site architectural support is unusual. There's a certain amount of stereotyping that architects have about tradespeople, and vice versa. But subcontractors come to the site with expertise in their fields, and then I come in with a broad understadning of the project to help put that all in context. The subcontractors were also surprisingly comfortable taking direction from me as a female. I even had my own port-a-potty out on site."
—*Nicole Starr, Architectural Project Manager*

"When I went out to Altamira to work as an on-site architect, I had such little knowledge about construction that it was a race to learn about something, figure it out, and try to do it. I was working on everything from laying out casework and joints in terrazzo, to figuring out how every single door was going to work, to detailing the titanium roofing. I worked side-by-side with the people that were installing the finishes. Once you know what they're capable of, it's a different ball game.

"It was the classic situation where the young architect is out there on site telling these seasoned craftsmen what to do. I tried to be sensitive to that dynamic. Of course, there were guys I got along with, and guys I didn't get along with. You hope for a perfect working environment, but that just doesn't exist, especially with the quality control element I was supposed to provide. I knew I had really arrived one day when I actually read my name in the wall of the porta-potty, and it was not flattering at all—aggressive stuff."
—*Brad Williams, Project Architect*

Unfolding as a series of views, the house gradually moves through the site and subtly breaks down the massive scale of the structure. The clients asked us to study a geometry that was more fluid, and less orthogonal than we typically design. This led us to investigate ideas about curves and interstitial spaces wedged between nonparallel walls. Based on site features and convergence lines, the walls of the house align to frame specific views of Inspiration Point, Long Point, Catalina Island, and other geographically significant locations. This sequence begins at the entry of the house and unfolds through the expansion and contraction of the walls. Only in the master bedroom is the entire panorama revealed.

The walls in the home had to have weight conceptually, as supports of this earthbound building, and structurally as retaining walls. Initially, we designed all of the walls to be exposed concrete. However, to create more texture, we decided to clad many of the walls in the local Palos Verdes stone. To soften the concrete walls, we added mineral pigments to the concrete mix for an earthier color and texture.

CLIENT INVOLVEMENT

"We were starting with a fairly unique site, so I knew whatever I put on it had to have a lasting relationship with the place. As a commercial developer, I knew I wanted to be the general contractor on my home, and in many ways, the project was at a commercial scale. Building with concrete and steel is the bread and butter of my business. In the end, at Altamira we poured 6,500 yards of concrete and used 890,000 pounds of steel. I am a land developer, so painting with a broad brush is very natural to me. I was most comfortable undergrounding the utilities and realigning the road. I also liked when we were drilling the foundation.

"When we started laying out the house, we really saw the impact that the nonlinear geometries would have on the building process. There is no trim in this house anywhere. No place to hide misalignments or take into account the different tolerances of materials. We had to resolve all of that in the details of the execution. I felt that having architects on site was like buying insurance that the execution would be as close to the design intent as possible."

—*Eric Johnson, Client/General Contractor*

Altamira was intended to be passed from generation to generation, so the materials and craft demanded a timeless quality. In many ways, the home was constructed like a commercial building, with steel structure and complex assemblies. Titanium roofing, concrete and stone walls, and floors made from terrazzo and hard wood create a tapestry of colors and textures that reveal their presence and permanence. Materials come together precisely in a constant desire for precise detail.

We had a complex working relationship with the owners on this project. As a developer by trade with extensive construction experience, the owner could act as his own builder, but he did not have the in-house staff to build such a large, complex project. We pulled from our own design-build team and provided construction support staff as well as full-time on-site architectural staff. This dynamic teaming was rare and allowed us to push each other to do the best possible work. Completing Altamira took as long as completing TAS. In both cases, we appreciate not only the completed structures, but the relationships we developed along the way.

INTERIOR DESIGN

"Our interiors team had to understand and embrace the organizational pattern of the house. The architecture comes together in a precise way, but at the same time the clients wanted to know where they were going to host their Super Bowl party. The wanted the house to last for the next four generations, so the furniture needed to live up to that expectation. Finding something that was luxurious but durable was the task. We had a lot of natural leathers that take on a patina over time. That slab of tree for the dining table obviously isn't going anywhere. We found that tree slab before the house was even framed. It sat waiting in the office for two years."

—*Daniella Wilson, Interiors Project Manager*

PALOS VERDES STONE

"I doubt I will ever see anything like Altamira again. The manufacturing of the stone on-site was such a big part of the job that it just seems unlikely anyone will ever be willing to invest that much effort and money into doing the stonework. The final stones they cut were just incredible. If it was a 2-inch stone, it was actually 2 inches. It was not 1 and 15/16, not 2 and 1/32. It was 2 inches. The edges were parallel with no taper, and the top and bottom of the face were at ninety degrees to the rest of the stone. I'm still amazed since it was a hand-sawn job—guys pushing stones through the saws.

"Once we had the stone, we just weren't quite sure what to do with it. We didn't really know how it was going to be in doing a whole wall and not just a little sample. We ended up laying the stone, putting the thin-set on the back, then slushing some mortar in since we didn't feel that the mortar alone would bond well enough to hold it. After figuring this out, we were able to slowly start adding masons to the job. We had trouble getting masons, and I know of a couple of instances where I made arrangements for masons to come to the site and when they saw the work, they just walked away because it scared them since the joints were quite tight. It was just so unusual."

—*Clive Christie, Mason*

Stone installation

132

CREATING A NATIVE LANDSCAPE
"My husband Eric and I both grew up nearby
and even had our first date right around here.
We always knew that we wanted to come back
to this area, so we were lucky to get this site.
We did a lot of work to keep it natural and
native. We have three acres of landscaping,
which is a lot of plants! We wanted to use the
least amount of water as possible. We love the
beach, so I made sure that we brought part of
the beach up onto our bluff. It is so fun and
cool to have these large sandy areas, which
also reduce the area that requires watering. On
the majority of the site, we only need to 'deep
water' the native plants once a month.

"I was very nervous when we were working
with the firm to design the landscape because
native gardens don't get a lot of water, so when
we would go visit native gardens, they looked
a little weedy and needy. But when they are
on your own site, you can take care of them.
I walk the site all the time and have learned
a lot about the landscape. My favorite plants
are our salvia because they are very pretty—
this awesome purple color—and smell very
good. We have humming birds, rabbits, rac-
coons, squirrels, and a breeding ground of
ladybugs. We have many little areas that are
different focal points around the landscape.
There is the pool area, three fire pits, volleyball
courts, lookout points, and a camping deck
that comes out of the sand."
—Susanne Johnson, Client

Before

FINDING THE RIGHT SITE

"When our real estate agent took us to the site where the Desert House is now, we were so moved by the relationship to the entire mountain range that created the valley. We put an offer in that day. No longer was the site relating to only San Jacinto peak, as is the case in Palm Springs, but this lot had a 360 degree relationship to the entire range of mountains. You could stand on the property and feel how the valley was formed. We also could buy five acres for a fraction of the price of the small infill lots in Palm Springs. We had an immediate sense of coming to the right place to do a modern prefab home."
—*Leo*

In a perfect storm of opportunities, our office became interested in exploring the potential of prefabrication right around the time that Leo and his wife, Alisa Becket, were starting to think about building a vacation home near Palm Springs, California. We knew that if we wanted to explore prefab housing, we needed to build a prototype. Leo and Alisa offered to be our guinea pigs and began looking for property specifically to do the prototype prefab house. In nearby Desert Hot Springs, they found an undeveloped five-acre lot with views of the entire Coachella Valley. The site fit the bill perfectly.

Though the house was going to be built in a factory, we began the process as we would any other residence—creating a design that matched the client's needs and site. We had no doubt that the home should open up to the stunning view down the length of the Coachella Valley, with the San Jacinto Mountains to the south and the San Gorgonio Mountains to the north. The site's other key feature was a slight rise in elevation coming up from the street that crested about half way down the lot. Ron did not want to perch the home on top of the slope and instead set it just below the rise to make it feel integrated with the land. We felt that somehow we could puncture the otherwise solid street side of the house to frame views of San Jacinto Mountain from the detached carport.

RESPONDING TO THE DESERT ENVIRONMENT

Deserts face vast temperature fluctuations, from freezing winter evenings to blistering summer days. To provide energy efficient ways of maintaining comfortable living conditions, we employed a host of passive and active designs. The Desert House derives a portion of its power from solar panels. Concrete floors act as a thermal mass that absorbs heat from the sun during winter days and radiates that heat back into the home at night. During summer months, the floors cool off at night and provide a stable temperature during the day. Deep decks on the south and west facades minimize the impact of the harsh summer sun, while triplepaned glass provides additional insulation against the heat and cold.

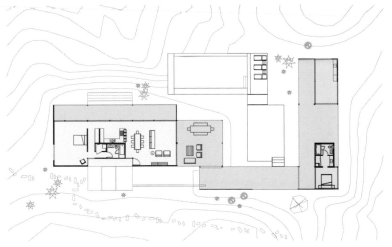

N
→

Floor plan

STEEL FRAME MODULES

Our early experience with prefabrication was in the very traditional context of school construction. At the LAX First Flight Child Development Center and again at The Accelerated School, we used prefabricated modules for classroom spaces. In 2003, Dwell magazine invited us to participate in the Dwell Home competition to design a modern prefab home. For the first time, we explored the use of prefabrication in a residential context. We dove into researching the different materials and methodologies of prefab. Through this research, we came to believe that using steel-frame modules was the best way to maximize factory efficiency and create an open, modern aesthetic.

From our firsthand experience as builders, we understood the inefficiencies of site construction, including rain delays, unresponsive subcontractors, runaway costs, and excessive material waste. We knew that if we were going to do prefab, we fundamentally wanted to fabricate everything possible in the factory. Panelized and kit prefab systems, where precut pieces or wall sections arrive to be assembled on site, never satisfied that requirement, for they still require significant on-site labor. We felt like only modular structures, where entire completed volumes of the house could be shipped to the site as a series of modules, allowed us the opportunity to preinstall virtually everything, from windows to flooring to plumbing to appliances.

Creating a significant sense of mass was important to prevent the house from getting lost in the expansive views and open site. We built up this visual weight by using concrete hardscape around the pool and fire pit area and creating extensive covered deck space. The elongated L-shaped plan extends the indoor and outdoor living spaces, forming a partially enclosed courtyard while visually blocking out the neighbors to the North.

From our previous work and research on prefabrication, we knew that we wanted to use steel frame modules as the core structure for the home because a modular system allowed us to maximize the work completed in the factory. We designed the house around a total of ten modules that are twelve feet tall, up to sixty feet long, and either eight or twelve feet wide. These standard sizes in factory production also simplified shipping requirements under the Department of Transportation.

In the interest of capitalizing on the standard practices in the prefab industry, we had the Desert House fabricated at a traditional prefab factory that typically makes schools and other commercial structures. We learned a great deal about plant operations and module fabrication, but we also saw the precise quality demands of modern construction push up against the limitations of traditional prefab production. Our in-house construction staff finished much of the building and installed interior finishes and custom cabinetry at the factory before the home shipped to the site. Then, in one long day, a massive crane lifted the modules off the flat-bed trucks and installed them on the stem-wall foundation.

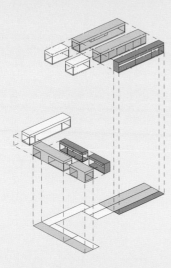

FIGURING OUT THE MODULAR SYSTEM

"I initially looked at the drawing set we did for the LAX Child Development Center and saw that the modules were twelve feet wide. That's really all we used in that early round of designing the Desert House since we wanted to have some form of design decided before we talked to any factory about production. We met with a few modular producers who gave us a drawing sheet here or there, but they wouldn't give me a whole set. It was enough to know what in general was happening, but when it got to details, inevitably there was not enough information.

"Once we selected a factory, the key was to use their standard modular system. We made small changes to our original design, like the thickness of ceiling structures, column sizes, and column spacing, to conform to their system. I worked closely with their in-house architect. The goal was to design and detail the structure in such a way that they could build what they always build, and before they knew it, they'd built a modern house. When you looked at the steel frames in the factory, you couldn't tell the difference between the Desert House and the school sitting right next to it.

"At the preproduction meetings, I would walk into the conference room where there would be twenty-five people at the table, including every lead in the factory. They would reserve the chair in the front of the room for me, and I'd sit down and think, 'Holy shit! I have to answer every single question that twenty-five people are going to throw at me.' They just weren't used to seeing that type of detail in construction drawings."
—*Jared Levy, Architectural Project Manager*

In two years, this prototype has become obsolete in many ways. As a prototype, the Desert House was an invaluable step toward developing our abilities to design and produce prefab homes. And in a good month, when not inundated by tours, it provides a bit of a vacation respite for Leo and his family.

Welding the structural steel frame

INSTALLATION DAY

"I will never forget the day that the house arrived. We were staying at a hotel down the road and were so excited, we didn't even sleep that night. The house was scheduled to arrive at four o'clock in the morning. Between three and four, I was awake and thought that every car that went by was our house. I didn't want to miss it. Every time something noisy would drive by, I would shake Leo and say, 'Our house is coming! We have to get up!'

"The ten modules were lined up on flatbed trucks, and it really didn't look like a house at all. It was just so hard to imagine that they would place all of the modules before sundown. They so efficiently picked them up—these huge sixty-ton boxes just dangling there from a crane—and placed them like a puzzle on the foundation. It felt like magic."
—*Alisa Becket*

"Most of the house modules had been set when the crew swung over to set the prefab carport roof onto the site-built columns. I was up by the house when all of a sudden, I heard a lot of commotion over by the carport and saw a group of people coming to find me. All I could think was, 'Uh oh.' They told me that the carport roof didn't fit. I went down there and sure enough, the welding plate on the carport roof did not line up with where we built the columns. A group of people were standing around, scratching their heads. There was a quick game of 'who screwed up' because having the crane there costs hundreds of dollars an hour. Should we leave it? Should we fix it? I opened up the drawings, and luckily it was not our mistake. The factory located the plate in the wrong place on the roof. Rather than forcing the issue of trying to make it work somehow, the factory offered to take the roof away to rebuild it and reset it at their own cost. I was so relieved because if it were my mistake, oh boy."
—*Jared Levy, Architectural Project Manager*

Open house, April 2006

PUBLIC RESPONSE
As our prototype home, we first opened the Desert House to the public in the Fall of 2005 when we launched Marmol Radziner Prefab. Our planning notes for the first open house said, "Attendance: 300–400(?)." We clearly had no clue what to expect, for we spent most of the open house in a state of shock as 3,000 people poured into the home.

"The response to the house has been over-whelming. People who have probably never responded well to a modern building are going into this very industrial environment and seem to genuinely appreciate it. Just go onto the decks, look up, and you see the screws and the corrugation of the metal deck above. There is nothing smooth and slick about it. I love going to the Desert House with my family, but because it was a proto-type, there has been so much public activity and action there. It's been fun to have such a positive reaction to the home, but someday it would be nice to have a small vacation house that no one cares about."

—Leo

FURNITURE

"The Desert House furniture was so successful because we had already done the Glencoe line and other custom projects, so we could draw from a really good vocabulary. This was particularly important because we did not have time to prototype the Desert House pieces. We had to design them, approve them, and produce them. A lot of the designs are Glencoe pieces reinterpreted in wood to be a little softer, a little more rugged.

"We wanted to design pieces that could be used inside and out. We also thought the pieces should be environmentally friendly and reflect the natural beauty and sparseness of the desert. We decided to use solid pieces of reclaimed wood that show their character. Also, reclaimed wood is well seasoned, so we could get away with using larger pieces that would be more stable."
—*Daniella Wilson, Interiors Project Manager*

Marmol Radziner Prefab

Previous spread: Installation in Las Vegas, Nevada (left), Prefab home in Moab, Utah (right)

A START-UP VENTURE

"It's nice to have control over the production, but it's also a huge capital investment. The first year of starting up the factory had every aspect of Marmol Radziner compressed into one real rollercoaster year: ballsy adventures, politics, bad decisions, good decisions, decisions we thought were bad that were actually good, decisions we thought were good that were actually bad, money woes, good design. All of it just condensed and strengthened. I'm proud of what we have built for sure, but I'm also anxious to see what's to come."
—*Brent Bryan, Cabinet Shop Manager*

With the Desert House prototype behind us and countless lessons learned, we started putting the wheels in motion to launch our prefab venture. Our first decision was to continue using a modular prefab system. Unlike kit-of-parts or panelized homes that ship flat and require significant on-site assembly, volumetric modules ship from the factory with everything preinstalled, thereby reducing the work required on site. We also decided to continue using interior and deck modules that are twelve feet eight inches tall, up to sixty feet long, and either eight feet or twelve feet wide. With these building blocks, we designed a series of model homes, ranging from one to three bedrooms, and developed a Website that allowed viewers to customize the materials and finishes for their model, with immediate detailed cost estimates and visual renderings for each design choice.

While we were enamored with the idea of selling small, relatively standardized homes, we quickly learned that, in reality, clients wanted to customize more than just the finish materials. Most wanted a custom home designed around their specific site and needs. In many cases, these "early adopters" had built a home before and knew the vast inefficiencies and headaches involved with site-built construction. They wanted a prefab home because it was quicker, more predictable, less wasteful, and less expensive than building a traditional high-end custom home. Because these are custom projects, we approach the design similarly to any residence—by understanding the nature of the site and the specific needs of the client. Playing with our standard module sizes, we strive to create homes that enable living in connection with the surrounding landscape.

We reflected on the Desert House and looked ahead to the production of these new homes. We determined that we did not know of any prefab factory that we felt comfortable working with to develop this concept of modern high-end prefab housing. In addition to full construction services for our site-built homes, we already had an in-house cabinet and metal shop that produced sheet metal, structural steel, and doors and

MAINTAINING PRODUCTION FLOW

"In typical construction projects, you're always under the gun of meeting the schedule, but you also face pressures from other factors. In prefab production, the schedule is the only gun that you're under. You can't dwell on problems. You need an answer, and you need an answer immediately because if you don't have the answer, you've backed up the production line and have a host of new concerns. With prefab, it's all about prethought and predesign. During fabrication, all that we and the architects do, in a design-sense, is look for the problems that are going to be five modules down the line so we can answer those problems first.

"Prefab is a very fast learning curve because it's like perpetual motion. It took a week to do our first structural steel frame, and then we got it down to making a frame a day. If you come up with a baseboard design or a new way to install casework, you'll find the results of that very quickly. To me, it's an incredible way of designing, and then bettering your design and bettering your design and bettering your design."

—*Jason Davis, Prefab Operations Manager*

First-floor module with staircase

Wood casework installation

Windows and doors installation

Stone floor installation

Module delivered virtually complete

Installation in Las Vegas, Nevada

WHY PREFAB? WHY NOW?

We see a number of converging trends that make prefab especially appealing at this moment in history. Particularly in the last three years, we have encountered an inability to accurately predict construction costs in an environment where labor and material costs were soaring in unprecedented ways. Prefab gives us a unique way to deal with the difficulty of accurately predicting future construction costs. Our interest in prefab grows from this context, not from an interest in prefab as an end in itself. We see prefab as a means of providing high-quality modern living spaces more efficiently.

At the same time, we are learning more and more about the role that buildings play in the degredation of our environment. Currently, residences consume one quarter of our nation's energy, and the average home construction process creates 8,000 pounds of landfill waste. By moving production into a controlled factory environment, we can reduce the waste produced in home construction through precise planning and the ability to reuse and recycle excess materials. Whereas excess materials typically are thrown into a dumpster, in our factory they go back into our inventory for use on the next home. Centralizing trades under one roof reduces vehicular emissions from travel to construction sites. We have also used the prefab homes as a tool to create a standard palette of sustainable materials, including Structural Insulation Panels (SIPs), low-VOC paint to Forest Stewardship Council–certified wood, recycled steel frames, and insulation made from recycled blue jeans.

windows, so we decided to expand our capabilities into operating our own prefab factory. How hard could that be? In many ways, we are now grateful for our naiveté. If we had known how challenging that task would be, we never would have had the courage to make that leap of faith.

Aside from choosing to work with a steel-frame modular system, operating our own factory has been one of our most important decisions in starting Marmol Radziner Prefab. Controlling the entire production process allows us to push the limits of how much is installed prior to delivery and therefore minimize on-site construction. Beyond the rough construction of mechanical, electrical, plumbing, and HVAC systems, the homes ship with essentially all of the finishes preinstalled, including stone floors, cabinets, tiles, windows, doors, drawer pulls, toilets, and appliances.

Similar to our decision of fifteen years ago to start constructing the homes we designed, bringing the production in-house has allowed us to produce our homes at the high level of craft that modern designs demand. Most importantly, our production and design teams can regularly sit down together and go through a project, detail by detail, to develop new systems and designs for producing the homes. While we're not there yet, we're working toward standardizing the elements that underpin our custom prefab designs. We hope the architectural staff will need to rethink fewer details with each new home and the production staff will not have to spend much time looking at the drawing set. Repetition of production—

Renderings for California prefab homes (clockwise from left): Palm Springs, Malibu, Summerland, Hollywood, Sonoma County

OUTDOOR LIVING SPACES

"I think having the deck module is the one thing that really sets Marmol Radziner Prefab apart. In the end, our prefab modules are boxes. You can design around it all you want, but they are boxes. We don't have all of the standard tricks of the trade of normal site-built architecture, where we can extend the roofline or set back a wall to create relief from the box. Having the negative space of the covered decks helps to balance the positive space of the boxes. It really was an important design move. People are really buying outdoor space, and many of our projects have more deck space than interior space. I think being outside in covered spaces is a better experience than being at grade on a wood deck or concrete patio. It's a more defined space, and yet you are still outside."

—*Jared Levy, Prefab Associate*

ENVISIONING THE DESIGN

"As architects, we design houses to take advantage of views and topography. Then, typically in site-built construction, we get to see a house unfold, slowly unravel as the foundations and walls go in. With prefab, we don't have the experience of having the house take shape and form on site. For example, I had been going out to the Desert House site for three months, and all I ever saw was a foundation. Then, finally, one day there was a house. I had wondered about all of these things, like will the facade cutout line up properly with the mountain or will the door frame the right view. Then all of a sudden, it was there in an instant. All of these questions worked out perfectly in the end. We now import topographic information into our computer models to ensure our designs accurately make the most of a site and its views."

—*Jared Levy, Prefab Associate*

the fact that when we finish one home in the factory, we turn around and start another—allows for continuous improvement of our designs and techniques. When we make mistakes, unlike with site-built construction, we get to make sure that we do not make the same mistake again.

Our current custom prefab clients all understand that we are still in a prototyping phase, trying out new structural systems, methods of fabrication, and designs. We hope that we can use this learning curve, this period of research and development, to design and produce even better custom high-end prefab homes. But we also hope to return to our original concepts of a more standardized product. With the overwhelming interest and the production efficiencies we have already seen, we cannot help but believe that a more standardized product, priced appropriately, could really change the housing industry.

COMPUTER MODELING

"When you're doing a prefab project, the priority of breaking it up into small buildings changes the way you think. We had to invent different ways of describing the house and find ways of breaking it up and tagging every aspect of it. We use a Building Information Modeling (BIM) program, which is really fun because it is like programming a building with very simplified code. You tell objects how to behave and assign the properties based on what they are actually made from. The project feels like it is already built once you model it in the computer. When I saw the photos of the house in Moab completed on site, I felt a little bit like it was already made a long time ago. That sounds presumptuous, but there is that feeling to it."

—*Gordon Stott, Prefab Architectural Project Manager*

"We were working with a client on an existing site-built house when the client saw the *Time* magazine piece on Marmol Radziner Prefab and asked us if we could prefabricate his house. Neither I nor Ryan Robinett, the other architect on my team at the time, had worked on prefab before. We got a quick introductory course on how modules worked, got the general idea, and were able to go with it. Because we already had an established library of prefab module frames, components, and details in our computer models, we could quickly transform the original design to fit our prefab system. This home became very complex and required a lot of research and development. Our office doesn't like to say 'no.' People here don't like to think they can't solve a problem."

—*Rob Kirsten, Las Vegas House Architectural Project Manager*

Renderings for prefab home in Venice, California

THE PUBLIC RESPONSE

"I talk to potential clients when they first contact us, answering their questions, understanding their site, and developing their architectural program and budget. Over the first year, people's questions evolved. At first the questions were: 'What? You're going to build my home in pieces and ship it to my site?' Then people came to know more about prefab and did their homework. Instead of asking basic questions, they started asking more advanced questions. I really get involved early with the client. The energy that's involved with that is pretty amazing. You get sucked into their dreams."

—*Brian Blackburn, Prefab Sales/Client Relations*

Prefab home in Moab, Utah

THE CREATIVE PROCESS

"After we bought this property and had our old house in escrow, I was working on the design for about a month and could not seem to resolve the main concept for the new house. I remember thinking, 'This is horrible! We're selling a really good home, and we're just going to have junk to live in.' I guess that's part of the creative struggle. When you are in the middle of it, you don't think you are ever going to get out. Now I like this design better than the old one."
—*Ron*

THE LONG FLAT SITE

In the eastern edge of Venice, we've now done three homes within two blocks of each other. These homes clearly relate from one to the next, as they are rooted in a similar context. We have also enjoyed watching the neighborhood develop a healthy stock of modern homes, with new designs springing up on many of the surrounding streets.

"Glencoe, Vienna Way, and another project that we are doing two doors down from Vienna Way all have very flat, thin, long sites that set forth similar problems. Our answers to those problems are very similar, with the building mass pushed to the edge of the site to maximize interaction with the landscape. It has a lot to do with the indoor-outdoor theme of living that goes along with all of our projects."
—*Stephanie Hobbs, Associate*

When a property that was twice as large came on the market just a block and a half away, Ron and his wife, Robin, decided to jump on the opportunity, sell Glencoe, and start on a new home. With their new home, Ron's family wanted to increase the interior and exterior play areas. Ron divided the site into thirds, with two facing plaster volumes bridged by a sunken kitchen. The southern structure begins in the front of the property and terminates in an outdoor dining area. The northern structure runs from the back of the property forward and terminates in an outdoor living area. In the center, a bronze metal box shapes the sunken kitchen that connects the two plaster volumes.

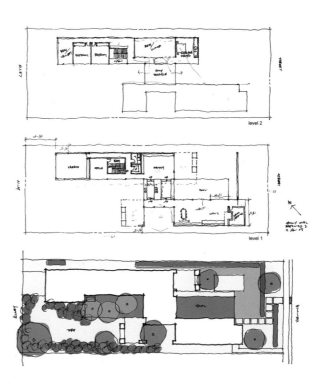

FROM NAPKINS TO A DRAWING SET

"Ron came to the table with napkin drawings—but complete napkin drawings, including plans, sections, and elevations. The initial plan is very close to what it is today. In terms of form and mass, the house is really straightforward. There are very strong datum lines that run through the building, and it's challenging to get different materials to line up properly. The pool also runs right up against the house, which makes it all the more complex. The house slab cantilevers around nine inches over the pool, so that the pool wall can come up flush underneath the sliding windows and doors of the building. Getting all of those alignments right was very tricky."

—Rob Kirsten, Architectural Project Manager

"When Ron and Rob Kirsten, the project manager, first approached our metal shop about the metal cladding, they made it clear that the panels had to be perfect. The kitchen had to seem like a metal seamless box, with the big plaster boxes smoothly sliding by directly on top of it. That meant the framing, waterproofing, and everything else that makes up the structure beneath the metal panels had to be dead on for it to all flush out.

"Initially, we thought there would be fifteen panels total. But once we saw the framing go up, we knew that there was much more going on. In the end, we had eighty panels. I spent two days with Dave Aylesworth, who heads our sheet metal shop, field measuring every column and fascia piece using laser levels and plumb lines. From these as-built drawings, we spent two weeks laying out the shop drawings for the metal. All of the panels had to be anodized to match the bronze finish of the windows and doors. Since anodizing can produce color variations between different batches, we knew we had to build once, anodize once, and install once for all of the panels to match. We did a dry fit of the panels to make on-site adjustments before sending them to the anodizer. I think Dave had nightmares where the panels came alive and attacked him."
—*Christian Munoz, Metal Shop Manager*

The one-story southern section houses a great room that combines formal living and dining areas. Conversely, the two-story northern section has more casual, private spaces, with a family room and office on the first floor and bedrooms on the second floor. In addition to bridging the two main volumes of the house, the kitchen is the center of a water-related area that starts in front with a swimming pool that runs the length of the great room, flows through the kitchen and over its green roof, and continues in the backyard's riparian landscape planted with rushes, reeds, and sycamore trees. These plantings give way to a large play space filled with buffalo grass and surrounded by Oak trees and other California native plants.

At the Vienna Way Residence, Ron pushed the ideas about mass, void, light, proportion, materiality, and the relationship to the landscape.

THE CENTRAL KITCHEN

The kitchen is no doubt the central hub of the Vienna Way Residence. It acts as the bridge between the public and private areas of the home and anchors the building in the center. To reinforce the transparency of the kitchen, the cabinets are all low, leaving the upper half of the walls completely free for windows. With the green roof above, nature seems to flow from the pool in front to the yard behind.

"The kitchen is always an essential part of our home. We like good, healthy food with produce from the farmer's market. With the sunken kitchen, the counter on the family-room side is at children's height, so they can very easily participate in cooking. We can also eat at the built-in booth in the kitchen, so we have more intimacy as a family than we had at the dining table at Glencoe.

"I really love how Ron designed the kitchen to be a pivot point in the house. The kitchen is its own, clearly defined, box that functions like the panopticon that Michele Foucault envisioned. While Foucault's concept of unobstructed observation was intended for prisoners, in our home we find the full views allow us to oversee the safety of our children's independent play."
—*Robin Cottle*

Synchronized swimmers at the National Trust for Historic Preservation cocktail party

THE FINAL HOURS

"We moved into the house while it was still under construction. For months, we were living in a three-ring circus with a continual flow of Marmol Radziner employees working on the house. Finally, the construction culminated in a flurry of activity preparing the house for its debut, a cocktail party for the National Trust for Historic Preservation.

"On the day of the event, people from every Marmol Radziner department were working to complete their tasks. Sofa cushions and books were spread all over. The coffee table was being constructed. The metal fabricators were installing the final touches to the facade. In the midst of it all, a synchronized swimmer jumped out of the kitchen window into the pool as she and her troupe rehearsed for their performance that evening. While the event was just a few hours away, I had confidence that we would all pull it together. Everyone was working with heart. In the end, the party went off without a hitch, and our home was complete at last."

—*Robin Cottle*

"I will never forget stepping into Ron and Robin's home the day before the cocktail party. The tranquility of the facade and entry pathway was counterbalanced by the internal madness and chaos, which an Easterner could only imagine is standard in Hollywood productions. I remember art handlers, book stagers, upholstery sprayers, landscapers, electricians, decorators with lamp shades rushing about. After wading through the sea of people preparing the house, I arrived in the kitchen to find Robin and her daughter happily eating a sandwich, as calm as a cucumber."

—*Christy MacLear, Executive Director of the Philip Johnson Glass House*

The textured individual spaces come together in rigorous relationships that were a challenge for our construction staff to build. Pushing up directly against the building, the pool runs flush to the wall of sliding glass doors. Not only did that necessitate our construction staff to integrate structural supports, radiant heating, and flush tracks for the sliders before the concrete pour, but it also required significant waterproofing preparations for the pool. As the first project where we fabricated the structural steel in-house, our own metal shop welded and erected the steel structure for the home.

After pushing through two nearly back-to-back construction processes, Ron's family is excited to be in their new home. Ron's young son used to say he missed having floor-to-ceiling windows, while in a rental during the construction, so he's happy to be "home" once again. They hope this home takes the indoor and outdoor living qualities of Glencoe and pushes those experiences ever further.

Williams Residence in Murrieta, California

Current Projects

While we still work on some renovations to existing homes, particularly mid-century homes, the majority of our current residential work is on new, ground-up, projects. Since we are essentially starting with a clean slate, we can focus on how each house sits in the landscape and uses the site as part of the design. When we approach a project, we spend a lot of time discussing how a building should interact with the land—will it float above the ground plane, like the Desert House? Will it sit directly on the ground plane, like the Glencoe Residence? Or will it nestle into the ground, like the Ward Residence? This primary decision enables us to best merge the building and the landscape in a site-specific way. We are also incorporating landscape design into the design process from the beginning so that we can develop the building form and natural surroundings in parallel.

Our desire for this natural connection to the landscape becomes particularly challenging on larger projects, where there is simply more building mass. Particularly on hillside lots, we try to mitigate the insertion of significant building mass by pulling the building apart into different volumes, often hiding mass by embedding it in the hillside. We do this not only to break up the scale but also to create adjacencies to the earth at multiple points in the house, thus strengthening the connection to the natural surroundings. As we work through these challenges, we are not surprised that some of our favorite spaces are often guest houses and pool houses. The ideas can remain pure in these smaller auxillary structures.

Residential projects are the core of our practice, but we are always looking to bring in work on commercial and community projects as well. On projects ranging from green yoga studios to child care centers, we try to integrate natural textures and materials. We bring in natural light, where possible, by enlarging windows and integrating skylights.

For years we have integrated environmentally friendly design into our projects. As we develop our early schematics for any project, we always consider natural ventilation, natural daylighting, passive solar design, and thermal massing. With the growing availability of sustainable products, we are able to incorporate green materials into more and more projects. From insulation to lighting, we are migrating our standard specifications to products that were created in a green way and provide long-term sustainability for the building.

As we focus on combining our designs with the natural environment, we have been fortunate to learn from some awe-inspiring artists and architects. Acting as the architect of record for several skyspaces by the artist James Turrell, we have seen how his work honed our sense of that which is not there—the sky, the light, and the colors beyond. When we work with James, we try to ensure that our architectural work silently supports his vision, as if our work is not there. Working as the architect of record and general contractor on two Tadao Ando projects, we now know more about cast-in-place concrete than we ever imagined. Building on our experience on Altamira and visits to Japan, we've learned how to improve our details and execution to produce highly refined architectural concrete that creates modern expressions of the material.

Constructing Ando's structures and our own technically advanced projects, we continue to develop our building skills. We try to improve our understanding of how buildings come together, wear over time, and can be built more sustainably. With ample space at the prefab factory, our shops have been able to grow in terms of their capacity and skill. We have brought more construction trades in-house, recently taking on structural steel and sheet metal fabrication as well as our own custom door and window shop. We hope that we are able to continue our trend of handling more and more trades ourselves in the quest to rise to the challenge of constructing the ideas that we imagine in our designs.

Project Credits

Altamira Residence, 2006
LOCATION Rancho Palos Verdes
TOTAL SIZE 15,500 square feet
CLIENT Eric and Susanne Johnson
PROJECT TEAM Nicole Cannon, Brian DeYoung, Meredith McDaniel, Olivia Erwin, Martin Fredrickson, Daniel Monti, Jesse Moyer, Brendan O'Grady, Laura Parisi, Jeff Pervorse, Sonya Reed, Bobby Rees, Susanna Seierup, Nicole Starr (Architectural Project Manager), Huay Wee, Brad Williams, Daniella Wilson, Ross Yerian (Construction Project Manager)

Chan Luu Retail Store, 2002
LOCATION Los Angeles
TOTAL SIZE 1,200 square feet
CLIENT Chan Luu Inc.
PROJECT TEAM Aaron Brode (Construction Project Manager), Brent Bryan, Reggie Dunham, Scott Enge, Stephanie Hobbs (Architectural Project Manager), Chris Lawson, Patrick McHugh, John O'Reilly, Jeff Tapper, Ross Yerian

Costume National Retail Store, 2000
LOCATION Los Angeles
TOTAL SIZE 3,100 square feet
CLIENT Costume National
PROJECT TEAM Reggie Dunham, Scott Enge, Stephanie Hobbs (Architectural Project Manager), Joey Sanchez, Nicole Starr, Huay Wee, Ross Yerian (Construction Project Manager)

Desert House, 2005
LOCATION Desert Hot Springs
TOTAL SIZE 2,100 square feet
CLIENT Alisa Becket and Leo Marmol
PROJECT TEAM Dave Bailey, Mike Green, Olivia Erwin, Jared Levy (Architectural Project Manager), Christine Skaglund, Carolyn Sumida, Huay Wee, Daniella Wilson

First Flight Child Development Center, 1999
LOCATION Los Angeles
TOTAL SIZE 10,000 square feet
CLIENT Los Angeles World Airports (LAWA)
PROJECT TEAM Paul Benigno, Paul Coleman, Anna Hill, Stephanie Hobbs, Iris Regn, Kari Richardson, Chris Shanley, Nicole Starr (Architectural Project Manager), Nathan Swift

Glencoe Residence, 2002
LOCATION Venice
TOTAL SIZE 2,800 square feet
CLIENT Ron Radziner and Robin Cottle
PROJECT TEAM Dan Caballero, Chris McCullough, Daniel Monti (Architectural Project Manager), Steve Passaro, Robert Renaud, Ross Yerian (Construction Project Manager)

Guttentag Studio, 1998
LOCATION Santa Monica
TOTAL SIZE 1,500 square feet
CLIENT Michael Guttentag
PROJECT TEAM Scott Enge, Teak Nichols, Brian O'Neill (Construction Project Manager), Iris Regn (Architectural Project Manager), Kim Sapida, Nicole Starr, Huay Wee

Harris Pool House, 1998
LOCATION Palm Springs
TOTAL SIZE 1,200 square feet
CLIENT Beth and Brent Harris
PROJECT TEAM Paul Begnino, Paul Coleman, Tim Day, Andy Kraetzer, Eric Lammers, Bill Matthews (Construction Project Manager), Chris Shanley (Architectural Project Manager), Jeff Wallace

Hilltop Studio, 2005
LOCATION Pasadena
ARCHITECT OF RECORD Thornton Ladd, 1950
TOTAL SIZE 1,300 square feet
CLIENT Anonymous
PROJECT TEAM Scott Enge, Gregg LaFortune, Chris Lawson, Scott Walter (Architectural Project Manager), Ross Yerian (Construction Project Manager)

Kaufmann House Restoration, 1998
LOCATION Palm Springs
ARCHITECT OF RECORD Richard Neutra 1946
TOTAL SIZE 3,200 square feet
CLIENT Beth and Brent Harris
PROJECT TEAM Jean Baaden, John Barone, Paul Benigno, Juli Brode, Jamie Bush, Peter Cohn, John Colter, Tim Day, Megan Dayton, Charlene Dekker, Scott Enge, Thom Faulders, Eliza Hart, Anna Hill, Stephanie Hobbs, Andrew Kraetzer, Eric Lamers, Eric Lawson, Christina Long, Bill Matthews (Construction Project Manager), Shauna McClure, Steve Neutzel, Teak Nichols, Alvin Pastrana, Tres Parson, Iris Regn, Chris Shanley (Architectural Project Manager), Sarita Singh, Mari Tsurimoto, Spike Wolff

Marmol Radziner Furniture Collection, 2003
PROJECT TEAM Brent Bryan, Scott Enge, Olivia Erwin, Anna Hill, Michael Ned Holte, James Mc Demas, Mauro Maya, Tony Monroy, Christian Munoz, Nancy Perlman, Hubert Plunkett, Lesley Roberts, Daniella Wilson

TBWA\Chiat\Day Offices, 2001
LOCATION San Francisco
TOTAL SIZE 27,000 square feet
CLIENT TBWA\Chiat\Day
DESIGN TEAM Paul Benigno, Juli Brode, Anna Hill (Architectural Project Manager), Michael Ned Holte, John Kim, Su Kim, Chris McCullough, Patrick McHugh, Daniel Monti, Brendan O'Grady, Bobby Rees, Rene Wilson, Annette Wu

The Accelerated School, 2005
LOCATION Los Angeles
TOTAL SIZE 110,600 square feet
CLIENT The Accelerated School
PROJECT TEAM Tracy Bromwich, Jim Burkholder (Architectural Project Manager), Nicole Cannon, Anna Hill, Stephanie Hobbs, Jeniffer Kim, Warren Bradley Lang, Risa Narita, Brian Nesin, Laura Parisi, Nicole Starr, Nathan Swift, Susanna Seierup, Annette Wu

TreePeople Center for Community Forestry, 2005
LOCATION Los Angeles
TOTAL SIZE 16,800 square feet
CLIENT TreePeople
PROJECT TEAM Paul Benigno, Nicole Cannon, Jason Davis, Susana Guzman, Eliza Hart, Anna Hill, Stephanie Hobbs, Daniel Monti, Brian Nesin, Teak Nichols, Laura Parisi, Bobby Rees (Architectural Project Manager), Susanna Seierup, Nathan Swift, Huay Wee, Jennifer Wilbur, Whitney Wyatt

Vienna Way Residence, 2007
LOCATION Venice
TOTAL SIZE 4,500 square feet
CLIENT Ron Radziner and Robin Cottle
PROJECT TEAM Brent Bryan, Olivia Erwin, Allison Gourley, Rob Tsurimoto Kirsten (Architectural Project Manager), Karin Lam, Jesse Moyer, Christian Munoz, Ryan Robinett, Shawn Wood

Ward Luu Residence, 2003
LOCATION Santa Monica
TOTAL SIZE 3,900 square feet
CLIENT John Ward and Chan Luu
PROJECT TEAM Stephanie Hobbs (Architectural Project Manager), Warren Bradley Lang, Marc Laughon, Juintow Lin, Patrick McHugh, Mike Meru, Michiko Murao, Brian Oxler, Jeff Pervorse, Sonya Reed, Daniella Wilson, Ross Yerian (Construction Project Manager)

Marmol Radziner Prefab
LOCATION Various
PROJECT TEAM Molly Bachelor, Carlos Barreto, Brian Blackburn, Brent Bryan, Herman Calderon, James Caldito, Kris Conner, Scott Enge, Jason Davis, Sam Fox, Gavin Grant, Eric Johnson, Rob Kirsten, Jared Levy, Richard Monugian, Karlo Munoz, Asaf Murdoch, Mike Patterson, Chris Pilgard, Riley Pratt, Ben Regnier, Tim Rich, Ryan Robinett, Erik Sollom, Peter Stokes, Gordon Stott, Christian Tamayo, Brad Williams, Atsunori Yokota

Photography Credits

Staff

MARMOL RADZINER + ASSOCIATES

Miguel Aguirre
Joseph Alguire
Adar Amador
Braulio Banuelos
Marisol Banuelos
Gabriel Banuelos-Perez
Deja Barlow
Romulo Barrientos
Enrique Barrientos
Armando Barrientos
Vilma Benitez
Gilberto Bittencourt
Carol Boone
Jim Burkholder
Raegan Brunson
Bruce Campbell
Alexis Carver
Gabriel Castolo
Lucita Charley
Meg Coffee
Elena Coleman
Miguel Contreras
Page Costa
Clay Courter
Eli Daniel
Brian Dassler
Alicia Daugherty
Robb Davidson
Lisa Day
Jose DeLuna
Matt Dente
Olivia Erwin Rosenthal
Gennady Fedonenko
Maria Godfrey
Ed Goldberg

Jackie Goldklang
Ruben Gonzalez
Allison Gourley
Ruth Greene
Sara Guerena
Ruben Guerra-Martinez
Richardo Hernandez
Stephanie Hobbs
Chip Howell
William Hsien
Fermin Hurtado
Lawren Jaccaud
Matt Jackson
Misty Kaplan
Chris Keller
Lucy Kelly
John Kim
Rob Tsurimoto Kirsten
Daniel Kramer
Kurt Krueger
Merrill Kruger
Karin Lam
Caren Lee
Ted Leviss
Jawn Lim
Albert Lucero
John Mack
Rhonda Mangrum
Olivia Manzano
Leo Marmol
David Martinez
Bill Matthews
Chris McCullough
Miguel Mendoza
Robert Mendoza

Guillermo Mercado
Jose Montoya
Julio Morales
Karen Morelli
Jesse Moyer
Amy Noles
Eamon O'Maille
Tisha Onada
Kevin Ormerod
Brian Oxler
Juan Pasando
David Pierson
Michael Poirier
Igor Pushin
Ron Radziner
Melody Rees
Katy Regnier
Courtney Rice
Arnold Rivera
Bruce Roberts
Luis Rodriquez
Joey Sanchez
Gregg Sanders
Chris Shanley
John Simon
Nicole Starr
Gorge Suares
John Wankner
Edward Webb
Karen Weise
Mindy Weiss
Shawn Wood
Annette Wu
Atsunori Yokota

MARMOL RADZINER PREFAB

Juan Aguila
Jose Jesus Aguirre
J. Chepe Alvarado
Orlando Archila
Oscar Ardon
Ruben Ascencio
Guillermo Avila
Daniel Ayala
David Aylesworth
Matthew Baker
Carlos Barreto
Mike Becker
Manual Anthony Benitez
Brent Bryan
James Caldito
Mauricio Carlessi
Roland Casey
Kris Conner
Francisco Corona
Ricardo Cuevas
Jason Davis
William DeLaVara
Alvaro Delgado
Kyle Derrick
Guillermo Elias
Kristine Estrada
Sam Fox
Dave Frala
Leo Gallegos
Eduardo Garcia
Jesus Gastellum
Scott Goldberg
Juan Gomez
Amilcar Gonzalez
Oscar Granillo

Alberto Gutierrez
Adolfo Guzman
Ricardo Hernandez
Jorge Ibarra
Benjamin Jaramillo
Todd Jerry
Brad Johnson
Juan Juarez
Jared Levy
David Lopez
Jonatan Lopez
Elio Martinez
Oscar Martinez
Mauro Maya
Gregory C. McCullock
James McDemas
Jose Medina
Gary Melnik
Marcos Menchu
J. Adrian Mendoza
J. Miguel Mendoza
Carlos Molina
Frances Monge
Tony Monroy
E. Antonio Montoya
I. Armando Montoya
Juan Montoya
Richard Monugian
Asaf Mordoch
Christian Munoz
Karlo Munoz
Robinson Nguyen
Cornelio Ochoa
Juan Olvera
Fran Pacheco

Mike Patterson
Duvanny Pineda
Omar Pineda
Hubert Plunkett
Riley Pratt
Gabriel Ramos
Steve Ramos
Ben Regnier
Carlos Reyes
Tim Rich
Jose Roberto Rocha
Abelardo Rodarte
Frank Rodriguez
J. Ernesto Rodriguez
Daniel Rogers
Jonathan Rosier
Andrew Roth
Juan Carlos Salcedo
Hector Sandoval
August Siement
Erik Sollom
Gordon Stott
Christian M. Tamayo
Christian X. Tamayo
Alfredo Urban
Juan H. Vigil
Ruben Villasenor
Noah Walker
Nigel Wallace
Brad Williams

With great gratitude and enduring respect, thank you to our clients, staff, families, and collaborators for their continual support of our work. A special thanks to Alisa Becket and Robin Cottle for their steadfast encouragement, patience, inspiration, and dedicated work, as we have grown our practice.
—Leo and Ron